# JUSTIFICATION AND ROME

# JUSTIFICATION AND ROME

by

## Robert D. Preus

**Concordia Academic Press**

A Division of

Concordia Publishing House

Saint Louis, Missouri

Copyright © 1997 Concordia Academic Press
3558 S. Jefferson Avenue, Saint Louis, MO 63118-3968
Manufactured in the United States of America

Library of Congress Cataloging-in-Publication Data

    Justification and Rome / by Robert D. Preus : edited by Daniel Preus.
       p.   cm.
    Includes bibliographical references.
    ISBN 0-570-04264-X
    1. Justification. 2. Lutheran Church—Doctrines—History. 3. Catholic Church—Doctrines—History. 4. Lutheran Church—Relations—Catholic Church. 5. Catholic Church—Relations—Lutheran Church. I. Daniel Preus, 1949-   . II. Title.
BT76435.2P74   1997
234 '. 7—dc21                             97–47476

   03  04  05  06  07  08  09  10  11      09  08  07  06  05  04  03  02  01

# Dedication

Dedicated to Donna Preus, whose faithful companionship,
constant encouragement, and love for orthodox Lutheran teaching
were indispensable to her husband, Robert

# Contents

# Selected Documents

| | |
|---|---|
| Book of Concord | *The Book of Concord: The Confessions of the Evangelical Lutheran Church.* Edited by Theodore G. Tappert. Minneapolis: Fortress Press, 1959. |
| *Catholic Catechism* | *Catechism of the Catholic Church.* Mahwah, NJ: Paulist Press, 1991. |
| *Condemnations* (CRE) | *The Condemnations of the Reformation Era: Do They Still Divide?* Edited by Karl Lehmann and Wolfhart Pannenberg. Minneapolis: Augsburg Fortress, 1989. |
| *Examination* | Martin Chemnitz, *Examination of the Council of Trent.* Tr. by Fred Kramer. St. Louis: Concordia, 1971. |
| *Justification by Faith* | "Justification by Faith," *Lutherans and Catholics in Dialogues VII.* Edited by H. George Anderson, T. Austin Murphy, and Joseph A. Burgess. Minneapolis: Augsburg, 1985. |
| *Loci Theologii* | Martin Chemnitz, *Loci Theologii.* Tr. by J. A. O. Preus. St. Louis: Concordia, 1981. |
| *On Justification* | "On Justification," Document No. 3, Fourth Assembly of the Lutheran World Federation, July 30-August 12, 1963, Helsinki, Finland. Studies and Reports. *Lutheran World,* Supplement to No. 1, 1965. |

| | |
|---|---|
| *Outmoded Condemnations* | *Outmoded Condemnation? Antitheses between the Council of Trent and the Reformation on Justification on Justification, the Sacrament, and the Ministry—Then and Now.* The Faculty of Theology, Georgia Augusta University, Göttingen. Tr. by Oliver K. Olson and Franz Posset. Fort Wayne, IN: Luther Academy, 1992. |
| Trent | *Canons and Decrees of the Council of Trent.* Tr. by H. J. Schroeder. St. Louis and London: B. Herder Book Co., 1941. |

# Foreword

Justification and Rome was the last written work our father produced before his unexpected death on November 4, 1995. Surely, the selection of this particular topic was providential. Is it not appropriate that the final scholarly effort of a Lutheran theologian should be on that topic of Christian doctrine which illumines all others and which, when death comes, gives to the Christian the confidence that he has eternal life?

The doctrine of justification gives us practical knowledge. Robert Preus was a practical theologian. Theology was the greatest love of his life because it revealed the love of God for sinners, and nothing could be more practical than the knowledge of God's love, which provides for a Savior who washes away sin and opens Heaven. Thus the study of justification is the most practical of all studies, for in no other article of the Christian teaching is God's love more clearly revealed than in this central article of the faith. The underlying motive for the writing of this study was that pastoral concern about the feeding of souls with the wholesome food of the pure Gospel which marked the author's entire life.

It is a timely topic. When it appears **to many** that convergence has occurred between Rome and the Lutheran Church on the meaning of the Gospel, the church needs a candid and competent analysis of the situation. This study does more than simply restate the respective positions of the Lutheran Church and the Roman Catholic Church of the 16th century when the polemical theological context yielded a clarity of doctrinal presentation on both sides. It also examines the pertinent materials of our generation on the same issues when the desire for consensus has led to language designed to obfuscate the doctrinal differences. Preus cuts through such obfuscation, explains clearly where Lutherans and Roman Catholics have equivocated, and, in the process, presents to the reader a succinct and honest evaluation of the current Roman Catholic doctrine of justification.

Robert Preus often opined that the key to teaching (and learning) dogmatic theology was to define carefully all of the theological terms. He shows how important this task is as he explains the differences in definitions between Lutherans and Rome on every significant theological term pertaining to justification. We are convinced that this study will clarify significantly the issues pertaining to this foundational doctrine. And even more important, we believe and pray that it will fortify the readers in their commitment and ability to express the precious truth on which the Church of Christ stands.

Daniel and Rolf Preus

# Introduction

The most important and vexing issue which has confronted Lutheran and Roman Catholic relations and discussions since the time of the Reformation is the doctrine of justification. It remains the major *status controversiae* separating western Christendom for over four and a half centuries. The debate and contention through the centuries over the doctrine of justification has not been confined to differences in the exegesis of a few Bible passages pertaining to the doctrine or to formulations of the doctrine, but to a fundamentally different understanding and conviction concerning the nature of the Gospel and the mission of the church. This fact explains the rationale and intensity of controversies revolving around the many doctrinal topics related to the doctrine of justification, topics such as original sin, the bondage of the will, repentance, confession, the atonement, sanctification, Baptism, and the Sacrament of the Altar. These loci and others are intricately related to the locus on justification and are inevitably affected by that relationship. It is significant that every article in the Formula of Concord, except Articles IX, XI, and XII, addresses doctrinal subjects which not only were contested among Lutherans but were treated by the Council of Trent. The Formula is almost as much a polemic against Trent and clarification of the Lutheran doctrine vis-à-vis Trent as a settlement of Lutheran controversies.

If all this is true, then a couple of compelling, operative conclusions follow. First, any attempt at rapprochement between Lutheran churches and Rome might well begin with a serious attempt to find consensus on the article of justification. Second, to establish true and meaningful consensus on the doctrine of justification will involve serious study of the topics of sin, Law, Gospel, redemption, repentance, Church, Sacraments, eschatology, and all the articles of faith which are integral to and interrelated with the entire body of doctrine. Confessional Lutherans would probably agree with these two operative conclusions and *modi operandi* in principle. Roman Catholics might agree that such a procedure is well advised if the two largest communions in western Christendom seriously seek doctrinal consensus or convergence or the less ambitious, but elusive, proximate goal of understanding each other. As a matter of fact, such a two-pronged procedure has been carried out, at least to some degree, in Lutheran/Roman Catholic discussions during the past decades.

The present study seeks to diagnose as precisely as possible the historic *status controversiae* between Rome and the Church of the Augsburg Confession on every substantive aspect of the doctrine of justification. It shall also venture to evaluate some of the various efforts of Lutherans and Roman Catholics to reconcile their differences and achieve consensus or "convergence" on the doctrine. The two primary sources will be the Canons and Decrees of the Council of Trent and the Book of Concord. The presentation of the doctrine of justification by the Council of Trent and the Lutheran Confessions represents the official and historic confession and doctrinal position of Rome and the Lutheran Church. Trent and the Book of Concord interact with each other. The Augsburg Confession and earlier Lutheran confessions react to the medieval scholastic doctrine of original sin, grace, repentance, sanctification, justification, and other related articles. The Tridentine presentation of justification was written in deliberate response to the doctrine of Luther and of Melanchthon in the earlier Lutheran symbols. The Formula of Concord, as noted, retorted in turn to the decrees and condemnations of Trent. And the controversy, articulated so succinctly by the two parties in the sixteenth century, has continued in its original form and style to this day. Since Vatican II the nomenclature has changed somewhat and the argumentation on both sides has been increasingly irenic, but all the issues separating confessional Lutheranism from Rome remain.

It is necessary, at the outset, to address the major issues in the historic controversy involving the article of justification and the related theological topics if there is to be an understanding and exposition of the article in its broad context. Presented first, therefore, are the Lutheran and Roman Catholic positions on the specific issues and theological topics relative to the doctrine of justification and then the reaction of each party to the position of the other.

# One

# The Centrality of the Doctrine of Justification and Its Hermeneutical Role

The article of justification, called the *articulus stantis et cadentis ecclesiae*, has always been given a prominent and central position and role in Lutheran theology. This is noted in the early confessions of the Lutheran Church. In the Augsburg Confession Melanchthon arranges all the articles of faith around Article IV on justification, and Article XX on "Faith and Good Works" presents the most extensive discussion in the positive section of the confession. In the Apology of the Augsburg Confession he calls the doctrine of justification the *praecipuus locus* of Christian doctrine, which, when understood rightly, illumines and magnifies the honor of Christ and brings to pious consciences the abundant consolation that they need. The German text adds that the article of justification serves for the clear and correct understanding of the "entire Holy Scripture," and "alone" shows the way to the unspeakable treasure and right knowledge of Christ, and "alone" opens the door to the "entire Bible" (Apol. IV, 2).

This statement of Melanchthon's indicates the role which the doctrine of justification would play in the life of the Lutheran Church, a role which took hold among Lutherans as they engaged in exegetical, dogmatic, and confessional theology, as well as in their preaching and pastoral care.

Melanchthon was only echoing a principle which Luther had already voiced and was to emphasize the rest of his life. Luther's most pivotal and best known expression of the principle is in his Smalcald Articles (II, II, 1-5) on the office and work of Christ, or redemption. He says,

> The first and chief article is this, that Jesus Christ our God and Lord, "was put to death for our trespasses and raised again for our justification" (Rom. 4:25). He alone is "the Lamb of God, who takes away the sin of the world" (John 1:29). "God has laid upon Him the iniquities of us all"

(Isa. 53:6). Moreover, "all have sinned," and "they are justified by His grace as a gift, through the redemption which is in Christ Jesus, by His blood" (Rom. 3:23-25).

Inasmuch as this must be believed and cannot be obtained or apprehended by any work, law, or merit, it is clear and certain that such faith alone justifies us, as St. Paul says in Romans 3, "For we hold that a man is justified by faith apart from the works of the law" (Rom. 3:28), and again, that He [God] Himself is righteous and that He justifies him who has faith in Jesus (Rom. 3:26).

Nothing in this article can be given up or compromised, [nor can any believer concede or permit anything contrary to it], even if heaven and earth and things temporal should be destroyed. For as St. Peter says, "There is no other name under heaven given among men by which we must be saved" (Acts 4:12). "And by His stripes we are healed" (Isa. 53:5).

On this article rests all that we teach and practice against the Pope, the devil, and the world. Therefore, we must be quite certain and have no doubts about it. Otherwise all is lost, and the Pope, the devil, and all our adversaries will gain the victory.

It is clear in this context that Luther is referring interchangeably to the article of redemption, upon which the justification of a sinner is based, and the article of justification. This is invariably the case with Luther, as with Melanchthon. One cannot fail to note that Article IV of the Apology from which the aforementioned citation of Melanchthon was taken addresses the propitiatory and mediatory work of Christ as directly as the article on justification by faith.

Furthermore, Luther uses the article of justification/redemption hermeneutically throughout the second part of the Smalcald Articles as he subjects the abuses of the papacy, prevalent in his day (the mass, chapters and monasteries, the papacy itself), to the judgment of the "first and chief article." If the teachings and practices conflict with this article, they must be abandoned, according to Luther.

But the article of justification serves not only to assess doctrine and practice in the church. It is the focal point and backbone, as it were, of the entire *corpus doctrinae*. And it is the basis of the Christian religion and life, for it is the very essence of the Gospel itself. Luther says:

This is the highest article of our faith, and if one should abandon it as the Jews do or pervert it like the papists, the Church cannot stand nor can God maintain His glory which consists in this that He might be merciful and that He desires to pardon sins for His Son's sake and to save.

If this doctrine of justification is lost, the whole Christian doctrine is lost.

This doctrine can never be urged and taught enough. If this doctrine is overthrown or disappears, then all knowledge of the truth is lost at the same time. If this doctrine flourishes, then all good things flourish: religion, true worship, the glory of God, the right knowledge of all conditions of life and of all things.[1]

To Luther the centrality of the doctrine of justification is essential to the work of the theologian, to his basic approach to theology and to God, to his carrying out the theological task, and to his own personal life of faith.

There is one article and one basic principle in theology, and he who does not hold to this article and this basic truth, namely, true faith and trust in Christ, is no theologian. All the other articles flow into and out of this one article, and without it the others are nothing. The devil has tried from the beginning to nullify this article and to establish his own wisdom in its place. Those who are disturbed, afflicted, troubled, and tempted treasure this article. They are the ones who understand the Gospel.[2]

This statement is not a piece of Lutheran hyperbole. To Luther it is precisely at this point, the doctrine of Christ and of justification, that the whole doctrine of God's Word, the *fides quae creditur*, contacts and reaches the person. For this article which is the essence of the Gospel bestows faith and fellowship with Christ, orients and directs the person theologically, and makes him a theologian. In his second disputation against the Antinomians he says:

The other articles are rather far from us and do not enter into our experience; nor do they touch us. . . . But the article on the forgiveness of sins comes into continual experience with us, and in daily use. And it touches you and me without ceasing. Of the other articles we speak as of something strange to us (e.g., creation, Jesus as the Son of God). What is it to me that God created heaven and earth if I do not believe in the forgiveness of sins? . . . It is because of this article that all other articles touch us.[3]

The article of justification actually enters the experience of a Christian, guides and even controls his theology and work, and helps to form, as it were, a theological *habitus* in him.

In my heart one article alone rules supreme, that of faith in Christ, by whom, through whom, and in whom all my theological thinking flows back and forth day and night. And still I find that I have grasped this so high and broad and deep a wisdom only in a weak and poor and fragmentary manner.[4]

For Luther the article of justification was not merely a key for reading and understanding the Scriptures and coordinating the articles of faith, but very specifically a bulwark for the confessing church, especially as it guards against false doctrine.

Therefore I say, as I have often said, that there is no power and remedy against the sects except this one article of Christian righteousness. If you lose this, it is impossible to avoid other errors or the sects. We see this today in the fanatics, the Anabaptists, the Sacramentarians, who having set aside this doctrine never stop doing away with other teachings, while erring and seducing others. And there is no doubt that they will raise up more heresies and invent new works. But what are all these things, even though they seem fine and very holy, compared with the death and blood of the Son of God who gave Himself for me?[5]

The centrality of the article of justification and its key function in exegesis, hermeneutics, confession, preaching, and holy living is not merely a quirk of Luther's which chanced to find its way into the theology of Melanchthon and the Lutheran Confessions at various points. It is rather a veritable and overarching principle which explains the theology and structure of Lutheranism. The article of justification—or the article of Christ (*solus Christus*), or of faith in Christ, or of Christian righteousness[6]—was soon called the *articulus stantis et cadentis ecclesiae* by all Lutheran teachers. These teachers regarded the aphorism not as a mere cliche, useful for polemics against

Roman Catholic theology, but as a fundamental, integrative principle in their theology, worship and practice, and in their ministry in the Church.[7]

One could hardly expect the Roman Catholic theologians of the sixteenth century to understand, much less appreciate, the position of Luther and the Lutheran Confessions on the doctrine of justification, especially their insistence on the fundamental importance and role of the doctrine. Luther's teaching involved a radically different understanding of the Gospel and of the Christian religion than that of Rome.[8] Luther had used the doctrine like a battle-ax to destroy the prevalent, public doctrine of grace, faith, penance, and sanctification in the Roman Church, as well as other adjunct articles of faith and various abuses. He had subsumed soteriology in its broadest parameters (including Christology) under the theme of justification (in the broad sense) and subjected all theology to the overview of this *praecipuus locus.*

It is unlikely that Luther's opponents in his own day and continuing long after the Council of Trent ever took seriously Luther's extravagant and radically new approach to the presentation of the Gospel which was so alien to their tradition and way of thinking. They did not even think to attack his assertion that the doctrine of redemption and justification was the chief article of the Christian religion, but only identified and condemned numerous "heresies" propounded by Luther and other Reformers. True, the fathers at the Council of Trent devoted much attention to the Lutheran doctrine of justification, but the reason for so doing was not that they felt obliged to reject the centrality or even the importance of the doctrine—the doctrine was peripheral to Rome—but rather that the Lutheran teaching on the topic undermined the Roman faith at many points of doctrine.[9]

After Trent there seemed to be little interest in the article of justification as such in Roman Catholic dogmatics, although the great Catholic controversialists, most of them Jesuits (Robert Bellarmine, Jacob Gretzer, Adam Tanner, Martin Becan, Thomas Stapleton, et al.), expended great efforts in writing lengthy disquisitions on the subject of justification in their defense of the theology of Trent and in their polemics against Luther, Chemnitz, Calvin, and other leading

Protestant theologians. That state of affairs has continued with just a few exceptions until Vatican II, which, significantly, with all its interest in rapprochement with "separated brethren," shows little interest in the doctrine which was so central to the Protestant Reformation. The two most popular manuals of dogmatic theology (at least in America before Vatican II, both translated into English and other languages and going through many editions), the *Manual of Dogmatic Theology* by A. Tanquerey, and *Fundamentals of Catholic Dogma* by Ludwig Ott, give almost no attention to the topic of justification, and when they address the subject, both repristinate the theology of Trent, with a few citations from St. Augustine and St. Thomas Aquinas interspersed.[10]

For four hundred years confessional Lutheranism has considered the article of justification fundamental to the proclamation of the Gospel and to the confession of the church. Rome has not. Except for their recent ecumenical negotiations with Lutherans, Roman Catholics scarcely talk about the article of justification. The doctrine is at best at the fringe of their *corpus doctrinae*, like a fingernail, or like the planet Pluto at the edge of our solar system, to use a different analogy. It's there, but no one has much interest in it. The term will not be found in the vocabulary of the average Catholic layman except in Germany and in the United States and other English-speaking countries where Lutherans and Roman Catholics live in proximity to each other. This is the situation today as Lutherans and Roman Catholics meet together and dialogue, work for doctrinal consensus, and strive to discern what really prevents these two communions from church fellowship and joint church work.

# Two

# Recent Dialogues between Lutherans and Roman Catholics on the Doctrine of Justification

A very brief survey of major dialogues centering in the doctrine of justification between Roman Catholics and Lutherans in the United States and Europe will help to set the present study in focus.

During the last thirty years Lutherans and Roman Catholics have come together in dialogue in a variety of settings. The results have been clouded. In 1963 the Fourth Assembly of the Lutheran World Federation convened at Helsinki, Finland, and hammered out a statement on the doctrine of justification. Roman Catholic observers were invited to attend as visitors. The statement entitled *On Justification*[11] is generic in nature and for all practical purposes ignores the Lutheran Confessions. The statement affirmed that the "image" of justification "stands in the center" of the many expressions used in Scripture to describe God's saving acts.[12] However, justification is only one "symbol" or "metaphor" among many metaphors and is a symbol which does not speak very well to our "existential" questions today, questions which are radically different from those of Luther—or the Roman Catholic Tridentine fathers, for that matter. Thus, the doctrine of justification as well as the term is seen as largely irrelevant today and, hence, has been marginalized. Ironically, the Helsinki capitulation was not to Rome, which politely stood by and watched what was happening, but to the historical-critical method of doing exegesis and to modernity. But Helsinki became the catalyst for a long series of meetings and dialogues between Lutherans and Roman Catholics over the years on the subject of justification, still an important topic to many Lutherans, but peripheral to Roman Catholics.

The next significant statement to appear after Helsinki was *Justification by Faith*,[13] which was the result of an unofficial but intensive dialogue between Lutherans and Catholics in the United States.

The participants found a number of areas pertaining to the doctrine where there were "convergences" and, like *On Justification*, pointed to "understandings," "insights," historical developments since the Reformation, etc., which did much "to overcome the confessionally and polemically based pictures of the past." But doctrinal unity, uniformity, and consensus were not attained, and the participants in the dialogue frankly admitted so.

It is significant that the Roman Catholic participants take occasion to discount specifically the centrality of the article of justification and its hermeneutical role, so emphatically stipulated and practiced in the Lutheran Confessions and later Lutheran theology. Their caveat is based upon the ruse that the principles of "Christ alone" and "faith alone," although Lutherans do not intend them to do so, endanger the means of grace function of the external Word, the Sacraments, preaching, and the ministerial office.[14]

Theologians from The Lutheran Church—Missouri Synod (LCMS) participated in the studies leading to the formation of *Justification by Faith*. The Lutheran Church—Missouri Synod, along with the Evangelical Lutheran Church in America (ELCA), was asked to respond and evaluate *Justification by Faith*. In 1992, "A Response to the Lutheran-Roman Catholic Dialogue Report VII Justification by Faith," was issued by the Commission on Theology and Church Relations of the LCMS. It was a mild and irenic statement in tone, but drew certain inescapable and predictable conclusions. The abject capitulation to the historical-critical method, the response stated, had relativized the concept of pure doctrine as well as the normative authority of Scripture and jeopardized the honest efforts of Lutherans and Roman Catholics to find any solid consensus on the article of justification. Also, "new modes of thinking," a kind of new logic, made doctrinal differences "not necessarily divisive."[15]

Such a bewildering conclusion in *Justification by Faith* no doubt springs from an ecumenical approach to theological conversations—an approach which marks all recent dialogues of Roman Catholics and Lutherans—rather than the older confessional approach typical of the Lutheran Confessions and the ecumenical church councils until Vatican II. The LCMS response scores *Justification by Faith* for concluding from an alleged "theological convergence" on certain aspects of the doctrine of justification that Lutherans and Roman Catholics have achieved "consensus in the Gospel." Actually, "consensus in the Gospel" was considered a given before the discussions between the Lutherans and the Roman Catholics ever began—a monumental *petitio principii*. Against the vague position of *Justification by Faith* the LCMS response insists that justification is a "critical principle" and "primary metaphor," not merely for distinguishing Christianity from other religions but for distinguishing and applying evangelical theology to the entire confessional and proclamatory message of the church. The response says:

> The dialogue, in our judgment, has failed to present the role which the doctrine of justification plays in Lutheran theology in its whole radicality. For Lutherans, this article is at the center of all the other articles of faith and it is at the center of each article. The doctrine of justification is the glue which holds the entire *corpus doctrinae* together, making Christian doctrine an undivided, an organic whole. It is the article from which all other articles flow and which all others serve. This is what makes Lutheran theology "evangelical" theology: it has the chief article of the Gospel, the doctrine of justification, at its heart. It is the article upon which the church stands or falls, and therefore, it is not, nor can it be, merely one metaphor among many (even if granted a "primary" role).

The LCMS response concludes with the words:

> Having reviewed carefully the "Common Statement" we have come to the conclusion that beneath the "differences in theological formulation" often noted, there remain substantive differences between the churches which go to the very heart of the Gospel itself and are therefore divisive.

It is understandable that the ELCA participants in the dialogue with Rome have publicly and loudly ignored Missouri's gentle and honest response and finagled Missouri's exclusion from further dialogues with Rome. Those who produced *Justification by Faith* simply did not understand the principle involved in the centrality of the doctrine of justification and, thus, failed to cope with the deep doctrinal cleavages still dividing confessional Lutherans from Rome.

Similar "ecumenical discussions" were taking place in Germany at the same time. These discussions were officially sponsored by Pope John Paul II and Bishop Eduard Lohse, chairman of the Council of the Evangelical Church in Germany. A joint commission was set up in 1981. An eumenical study group consisting of able Roman Catholic and Protestant scholars was formed. In 1985 their conclusions were published in a document, edited by Karl Lehmann (Roman Catholic) and Wolfhart Pannenberg (Lutheran), with the provocative title, *The Condemnations of the Reformation Era, Do They Still Divide?*[16] (CRE). The conclusions drawn are highly significant. Due to alleged new insights and breakthroughs in biblical and historical studies, the condemnations of the Lutheran Confessions and the Council of Trent are today viewed as either beside the point or obsolete and inapplicable and irrelevant to today's situation. Thus, the subject of the prominence and hermeneutical role of the doctrine of justification was not broached and the matter was ignored.

Such a sweeping conclusion was bound to be challenged. The challenge was ably presented by the Theological Faculty of Georgia Augusta University, Göttingen, in a study entitled *Outmoded Condemnations?* translated into English and published in the *Lutheran Quarterly* in 1991.[17] The Göttingen statement takes issue with the approach, the methodology, and the conclusions of *Condemnations of the Reformation Era* at every point. The condemnations of Trent and the Lutheran Confessions are still pertinent and to the point and continue to establish a *status controversiae* which still obtains between Lutherans and Roman Catholics, according to *Outmoded Condemnations*. The historical-critical method and all new exegetical and historical "insights" notwithstanding, the differences on the doctrine of justification between the Lutheran Church and the Roman Catholic Church still exist on such topics as original sin, concupiscence, bondage of the will, human passivity in conversion and justification, grace, *sola fide* and good works, and the assurance of salvation.

If the critique of the LCMS response to *Justification by Faith* and of *Outmoded Condemnations?* to *The Condemnations of the Reformation Era* are only half right, then the efforts both in America and Germany to find meaningful consensus in the doctrine of justification have failed. The efforts which produced *Justification by Faith* and *The Condemnations of the Reformation Era* have been motivated and driven by ecumenical and, on the part of Rome, ecclesiastical considerations rather than a specifically focused agenda to settle past important controversies and achieve real consensus on the doctrine of the Gospel and the article of justification.

The most recent, and without question the most important, attempt to settle past controversies on the doctrine of justification and establish consensus upon which mutual recognition of fellowship can be established between Roman Catholics and Lutherans has been made under the auspices of the Rev. Ishmael Noko, General Secretary of the Lutheran World Federation, and the Rev. Edward Idris Cardinal Cassidy, President of the Pontifical Council for Promoting Christian Unity—apparently with official papal approval. The document is entitled *Joint Declaration on the Doctrine of Justification between the Lutheran World Federation and the Roman Catholic Church* (hereafter *Joint Declaration*).*

*Joint Declaration* is not an original study but has been candidly drawn from the arguments and conclusions of *Condemnations of the Reformation Era, Justification by Faith,* and other documents of lesser importance. No recognition is given to the LCMS response to *Justification by Faith,* to *Outmoded Condemnations,* or to any study critical of *Condemnations of the Reformation Era* and *Justification by Faith.* The authors of the draft are anonymous.

---

*In his original manuscript completed during the autumn of 1995, Robert Preus had included the following statements: "*Joint Declaration* has not yet been officially released, and above its title appear the words, 'not for quotation or publication.' However, the existence of the document is common knowledge and, with the aid of FAX and E-mail, copies of it have been sent all over the world. In the present study we cannot ignore the document and its contents, but we shall honor the restrictions imposed by its sponsors and not quote directly from it." Since Preus wrote these words, the document has received rather wide distribution. After final revision by the Standing Committee for Ecumenical Affairs of the Lutheran World Federation it will be submitted to member LWF churches for their response. Final approval of the document is expected by December 31, 1998, at the latest.

The conclusions of *Joint Declaration* are remarkable and go further than previous studies and statements. Not just convergences exist, according to *Joint Declaration*, but actual consensus and a common understanding between Lutherans and Roman Catholics of the faith content of the doctrine of justification. Like *Justification by Faith,* no condemnations are directed against the historic Lutheran or Roman Catholic position; and *Joint Declaration,* following *The Condemnations of the Reformation Era,* finds all antitheses inappropriate in our modern situation. Like *Justification by Faith, Joint Declaration* dialectically presents a fairly accurate description of the Lutheran position on pertinent points alongside the Roman Catholic position, but presents them not as antithetical but as complementary to each other. Recognition is given to the fundamental priority of justification in the Lutheran Confessions. Equal acknowledgment is accorded the Roman Catholic position which taught a doctrine of justification quite different in character (a process of sanctification) and treated the forensic doctrine of justification, affirmed in the Lutheran Confessions, as a peripheral aspect of salvation by grace. Neither the fact of the sinner's justification before God for Christ's sake nor the article of justification in the scheme of Christian doctrine and the church's proclamation is given any hermeneutical role for exegesis, confession, or practice.

# Three

# The Basic Structure of the Article of Justification

The Lutheran position on a number of salient aspects and constitutive parts of the doctrine of justification according to the Lutheran Confessions needs to be compared with the doctrine of Trent and Roman Catholicism since Trent. Such a procedure is imperative to understand and evaluate properly the recent Lutheran/Roman Catholic dialogues which have taken place and the statements which have resulted from these meetings.

But before embarking on such a prospect, one historical observation about the structure of the Lutheran doctrine of justification needs to be pointed out. This observation is based on solid historical data and should be acceptable to both Roman Catholics and Lutherans alike, as they study and evaluate the historic Lutheran doctrine.

From the very first the Lutheran doctrine of justification has been reduced to the following classical summary formulation: a sinner (1) is justified [saved] (2) by grace, (3) for Christ's sake, (4) through faith (5). This brief aphorism encapsulates the entire presentation of Apology IV "On Justification." Melanchthon (Apol. IV, 214) says, "We believe and teach that we are accounted righteous before God for Christ's sake by faith." The Council of Trent rejected this formulation as it stood in the sense in which the Lutheran Confessions meant each key word or phrase in the formulation. The Tridentine fathers meant something different from the Lutheran confessors in respect to every term and phrase in the formulation. They understood and defined and described sin differently, grace differently, justification differently, Christ's saving work in relation to justification differently, and the function, or role, of faith in the justification of the sinner differently.

In theory and formally Trent could have accepted the formulation, but only by putting Roman Catholic content into each chief term and concept. Such a procedure has actually been carried out by Roman Catholic theologians from time to time, especially in recent years. Nor is there anything intrinsically wrong with a procedure which follows—or at times leads into—the development of language and semantic change which in the longer term is inevitable.

The history of doctrine is filled with instances of terms changing their meaning over a span of time, sometimes quickly. The ecclesiastical terms "merit" and "satisfaction" were given a completely new evangelical meaning by Luther and the Lutheran Confessions. The biblical terms "grace," "faith," and "justification" were rehabilitated by the Lutherans according to their biblical signification and intention.

*Equivocation* is what happened, however, between Lutherans and Roman Catholics as they debated the doctrine of justification—massive equivocation. Both parties recognized that downright equivocation lurked behind every phrase and term in their respective formulations of the doctrine. Yet each side deliberately and doggedly defended its understanding and definition of the commonly used terms. Each side recognized that the *status controversiae* in the article of justification centers in the radically different meaning attached by each side to the terms and concepts common to both sides. In fact, this was the controversy: plain and outright disagreement about what was meant by sin, grace, justification, the *propter Christum*, and faith (*sola fide*). Each party knew full well that to forfeit its definitions was to forfeit its doctrine and confession.

The same fundamental equivocation in respect to the basic terms relative to the doctrine of justification still exists today between Lutherans and Roman Catholics. However, these equivocations and ambiguities are used in a radically different fashion today. In the sixteenth and following centuries the equivocations were used to point up and clarify the *status controversiae* and to enable each party to argue and defend its position more effectively. In the last fifty years the climate in which doctrinal controversies are addressed has changed radically. Polemics has given way to an irenic approach whereby all controversies are absolved or dissolved rather than resolved. All the former historic equivocation obtains and is still out in the open. However, equivocation is no longer seen as a basic difference in meaning and definition which points to a real and honest doctrinal difference, but rather as a non-divisive and fruitful difference of "understanding," "interpretation," "emphasis," or "insight" which actually enhances the overall composite Lutheran/Catholic doctrine of justification. As a result, equivocation is no longer a barrier to doctrinal consensus, mutual recognition, and ecclesiastical cooperation and fellowship. Rather it has become a positive aid in bringing about these noble goals. A whole new agenda and *modus operandi* in ecclesiastical dialogue and doctrinal discussions have been established by the facile equivocation of the concept of equivocation.

But it is time, without more prolegomenous remarks, to turn to the discussion of the aspects and parts of the doctrine of justification which through the centuries have distinguished and separated the church of the Augsburg Confession from the church of Rome and of Trent. What specifically are these points of doctrine which have been an obstacle to consensus and fellowship? Have they in recent times been bridged? Have the old doctrinal differences been settled? The five essential aspects and elements of the doctrine of justification are those constituting the formulation mentioned above: a sinner (1) is justified [saved] (2) by grace, (3) for Christ's sake, (4) through faith (5).

# Four

## The Context of the Doctrine of Justification

There is no context for the Triune God, no *principium essendi.*[18] God is His own context and *principium essendi.* Our Triune God—and each person in the Holy Trinity—is, as Athanasius and the Eastern Fathers put it, *autotheos* (*in se ipso Deus est*), each divine person possessing the entire Godhead. There is, likewise, no context and no *principium essendi* for the interpersonal relationships (*actiones Dei ad intra personales*) of God. He is the total and only source and context for His *opera ad intra.*

The external acts of God, His *opera ad extra,* however, have a context. And these external acts of the Trinity can be known and understood only in the light of their background and context. God Himself provides the context for His acts of creation, of providence, of judgment and grace, and also of our understanding and relationship to these mighty acts. As our old Lutheran dogmaticians put it, God is the *principium essendi* of all theology, and His Word of revelation in Scripture is the *principium cognoscendi* of all true and saving theology.

What does all this have to say to the fact—and to the doctrine—of the sinner's justification before God? According to God's revelation in Scripture, the context of the sinner's justification before God is the following. God, out of His infinite power and benevolence, created all things. Man was the crown of His creation, made in His own image, fearing, loving, and trusting in God above all things, and knowing Him as his loving Father and Creator. But man (Adam and the whole human race) rebelled against God, fell into sin, and lost the divine image. Man, therefore, became God's enemy, the object of God's wrath and subject to God's judgment, and in utter need of salvation and forgiveness.

Then God, in His infinite grace, took action. He sent His Son, who was the radiance of His glory and the express image of His person (Hebrews 1:3), to become man (John 1:14), and to redeem the world (Galatians 4:4) and restore it to glory and communion with Him (John

3:17). For Christ's sake God, who was angry with the sinful world, was reconciled, propitiated, and at peace with the world (1 John 2:2; Luke 2:14).

These are the facts, the realities, which serve indispensably as the context for the justification of a sinner before God. Luther has caught the gist of what has happened in his magnificent hymn:

> But God beheld my wretched state
> Before the world's foundation,
> And, mindful of His mercies great,
> He planned my soul's salvation.
> A father's heart He turned to me,
> Sought my redemption fervently:
> He gave His dearest Treasure.

The justification of a sinner before God can be considered either as an *action* of God whereby He declares the sinner righteous, or as an *article of faith* to be taught and preached in the church and in the world. In either case the same context and presuppositions obtain. The fact and reality of man's sin and God's grace and redemption of the world are the presuppositions for God's act of justifying the sinner. The articles of sin and grace, Law and Gospel, are the underlying context for preaching and teaching the Gospel of justification. And the article of justification cannot be understood apart from the vantage point of man's sin and God's grace. The article of justification cannot be taught or received in a vacuum.

These truths concerning the underlying background and context of the article of justification represent the common conviction of Lutherans and Roman Catholics, except that Rome would probably today claim other sources for revealed theology than Scripture alone. This agreement, extremely significant in its scope, has been used to great advantage by participants in modern dialogues between Roman Catholics and Lutherans.

Another area of notable agreement between Roman Catholics and Lutherans of the sixteenth century pertaining to the context for the doctrine of justification, however, has not been generally recognized nor made use of. This agreement centers in the fact that both Lutherans and Roman Catholics in their confessions and in their positive theology have held to the historicity of man's fall into sin and the reality of man's subsequent depravity and guilt before God. Both sides have held that God is really the "Creator of heaven and earth, and of all things visible and invisible." They have believed that the incarnation, Christ's vicarious death, His resurrection, and other redemptive acts are not mere "symbols" (Tillich) or "myths" (Bultmann) or "faith events" (G. Ernest Wright), but real, saving events within history. They did not speak of God's act of justification as a mere idea or theological construction, something fictitious, meta-historical, or unreal, to be expressed only by surreal pictures and irreducible metaphors (*On Justification, Justification by Faith, Joint Declaration*). Rather, they saw it grounded in reality, the stark reality of man's fall into sin and loss of the divine image, of his guilt (*reatus*) before God and of God's anger and judgment, but then also the blessed reality of God's mercy and Christ's atonement for the sins of the world.

All these basic truths were the common belief of Lutherans and Roman Catholics in the sixteenth century and were assumed in their confessions. And this seems to be the case also today among Lutherans and Roman Catholics, at least among those who take their doctrine and confessions seriously.

It is in *their understanding and definition* of commonly used words and terms and theological concepts that Lutherans and Roman Catholics differ from each other, sometimes radically. Such divergences in understanding and definition often result in equivocation and real doctrinal differences. To arrive at doctrinal consensus and a common confession of faith, words and terms and theological concepts must be used by both parties in the same sense and defined unequivocally. Is this the case? An examination is in order of the key terms and phrases composing the Lutheran doctrine of justification cited above in an attempt to understand what Lutheranism meant by these terms and phrases and how Rome has reacted to the Lutheran understanding.

# Five

## Sin

The Lutheran doctrine of sin is centered in the Article on Original Sin—in the portrayal of man's fallen, sinful nature, rather than in the article of actual sins which a person commits daily. In fact, there is no specific article on actual sin in the Lutheran Confessions. Sin has its origin in real history. "Since the fall of Adam all men who are born according to the course of nature are conceived and born in sin" (Augsburg Confession II, 1). All men are, therefore, sinful by inheritance (*Erbsünde*). What is the nature of man's innate sinfulness? *Negatively*, man is without fear toward God and trust in God. The Roman Confutation disagreed with this definition. The Confutation maintained that to be without fear and trust in God is the *actual guilt* of adults rather than of infants who do not possess the full use of reason.[19] *Positively*, Melanchthon defined original sin in the Augsburg Confession as concupiscence, the active inclination toward evil.

> When righteousness is lost, concupiscence follows. Since nature in its weakness cannot fear and love God or believe in Him, it seeks and loves carnal things; either it despises the judgment of God in its security, or it hates Him in its terror. . . . Concupiscence is not merely a corruption of the physical constitution, but the evil inclination of man's higher capacities to carnal things. (Apology of the Augsburg Confession II, 24; hereafter Apology)[20]

Again the adversaries, following the medieval scholastic theologians, took exception, saying that concupiscence in itself is not sin, but rather is just a penalty for sin.[21] One of the results and fruits of sin is concupiscence. The Council of Trent (hereafter Trent) affirms,

> This concupiscence, which the Apostle sometimes calls sin, the Holy Council declares the Catholic Church has never understood to be called sin in the sense that it is truly and properly sin in those born again, but in the sense that it is of sin and inclines to sin. But if anyone is of the contrary opinion, let him be anathema. (Trent, Ses. V, Par. 1)[22]

Melanchthon had already replied to this objection (Apology, II, 47), saying that, of course, both the deficiency of original sin, namely, lack of fear and trust toward God, and the concupiscence of original sin may be rightly called a punishment from God; but they are also sin against God. Previously he had stated his position even more graphically in his *Loci Communes* of 1521.

> Original sin is a sort of living power [*vivax quaedam energia*] in no way and at no time bringing forth any other fruits than vice. For when does the soul of man not burn with evil desires, desires in which even the most base and offensive things are not checked? Avarice, ambition, hatred, jealousy, rivalry, the flames of lust, wrath; and who does not feel these things? Pride, scorn, pharisaic big-headedness, contempt of God, distrust of God, blasphemy. But the most noble affections few people feel. True, there are those who live honorable lives outwardly, such as Paul who testified that he lived in such fashion before he knew Christ; and no one could find fault with him. But such persons have no reason to glory, for their souls are subject to the most base and miserable affections while they are not even aware of the fact.[23]

To Melanchthon and the other Lutheran reformers original sin was an active desire (*morbos*), a power which has completely corrupted our human nature (Formula of Concord, Solid Declaration I, 5); original sin was a condition. It is what Luther called the "root sin" (*Hauptsünde*). It is the source of all evil actions which oppose the Ten Commandments (Smalcald Articles III, 1-2), a power which is never inactive or at rest.

This awful description of man's condition is no academic point in Lutheran theology, but affects the articles of repentance, justification, the Sacraments, and the other articles of faith. In fact, it affects the whole course of the Christian's life of faith. The child of God can never rid himself of the flaming *fomes* and concupiscence of original sin. Baptism forgives our original sin and sinfulness, but does not eradicate it. The child of God is still a sinner by nature. In this life he is never rid of his concupiscence (Apology IV, 169). Luther points out that when a sinner is justified, his sin and flesh are not completely eradicated, but rather forgiven, not counted against him. Luther puts the matter very succinctly in the Smalcald Articles (III, XIII, I) as he discusses the article of justification. He says,

I do not know how I can change what I heretofore constantly taught on this subject, namely, that by faith (as St. Peter says) [Acts 15:9] we get a new and clean heart and that God will and does account us altogether righteous and holy for the sake of Christ our Mediator. Although sin in our flesh has not been completely removed or eradicated, He will not count or consider it (*rechnen noch wissen*).

God's forgiveness in Baptism, in the Lord's Supper, in absolution, and in the Gospel Word takes away the guilt and punishment of sin, but the power of sin is never completely broken in this life. "Baptism removes the guilt of original sin, even though concupiscence remains" (Apology II, 35).[24] Every Christian, therefore, while he remains forgiven, saved, and justified only for Christ's sake and by God's grace alone, at the same time remains a sinner, guilty before God, and in constant need of forgiveness, salvation, and God's grace.

# Six

# The Bondage of the Will

Correlative to the Lutheran doctrine of sin is the Lutheran teaching on the bondage of the will, articulated by Luther in his celebrated *De Servo Arbitrio*.[25] In this diatribe against Erasmus Luther treats the topic of the free will of the natural man from the perspective of the biblical doctrine of sin, not out of any philosophical considerations. The confessional Lutheran position was stated emphatically as follows:

> It is evident, as we have pointed out at greater length in the article on original sin (to which for the sake of brevity we only refer), that the free will by its own natural powers can do nothing for man's conversion, righteousness, peace, salvation, cannot cooperate, and cannot obey, believe, and give assent when the Holy Spirit offers the grace of God and salvation through the Gospel. On the contrary, because of the wicked and obstinate disposition with which he was born, he defiantly resists God and His will unless the Holy Spirit illumines and rules him. (Formula of Concord, Solid Declaration II, 18)

One cannot fail to see that the article on the bondage of the will corresponds in both its negative side and its positive side with the Lutheran doctrine of original sin. In fact, so totally has original sin "poisoned us from the sole of our feet to the crown of our head" (Formula of Concord, Solid Declaration I, 62),[26] so thoroughly is man before and after his conversion enmeshed by concupiscence (Apology II, 26; XVIII, 5) which remains also after baptism and conversion (Apology II, 35), that the unregenerate man sins even when he performs "outwardly civil works" and "produces deeds that are excellent and praise worthy in his own eyes" (Apology IV, 33). And he affronts Christ thereby (Apology IV, 24). Furthermore, even the good works of the believers are imperfect and impure (Formula of Concord, Solid Declaration IV, 21; cf. Augsburg Confession XX, 40).

The confessional Lutheran doctrine of original sin as worked out in the Apology and by Luther in the Smalcald Articles and the doctrine of the Bondage of the Will in Luther's *De Servo Arbitrio* and later in

Article II in the Formula of Concord are presented in deliberate antithesis to the doctrine of the scholastics and the common Roman Catholic theology of the day. Rome reacted immediately. But the conclusive response was given by Trent (Session V). And in Session VI on justification the Lutheran doctrine of the bondage of the will of the unregenerate man in spiritual matters was unequivocally condemned (Trent, Ses. VI, Canon 4); so also Luther's teaching that in conversion the will of man is "merely passive" (*pure passive*) (Formula of Concord, Solid Declaration II, 85), a point which was basic to Luther's doctrine. Moreover, the confessional Lutheran belief that the most noble works of unbelievers and the attempts of unbelievers to please God are an abomination and an affront to Christ is categorically condemned by Trent.

# Seven

# Repentance

The realistic doctrine of original sin—Melanchthon contends with St. Augustine that the inclination (*fomes*) to evil is not something neutral (*adiaphoron*), but is "truly sin" (*vere peccatum*) (Apology II, 42)—leads the Lutheran reformers to a new and completely different notion and practice of repentance, a revolutionary notion, already articulated in Luther's 95 Theses and a direct cause of Pope Leo X's excommunication of Luther (*Exurge Domine*) in 1520. The Lutheran Confessions develop and defend this new doctrine of repentance which is a return to the correct understanding of the New Testament meaning of *metanoia*.

What then is the Lutheran doctrine and practice of repentance? Luther explains in the Smalcald Articles (SA III, III) after his treatment of sin (original sin) and Law.

> The chief function or power (*Ampt oder Kraft*) of the Law is to make original sin (*Erbsünde*) manifest and to show man to what utter depths his nature has fallen and how corrupt it has become. So the Law must tell him that he neither has nor cares for God or that he worships strange gods—something that he would not have believed before without a knowledge of the Law. Thus, he is terror stricken and humbled, he becomes despondent and despairing, anxiously desires help but does not know where to find it, and begins to be alienated from God, to murmur, etc. This is what is meant by Romans 4:15, "The Law brings wrath," and Romans 5:20, "Law came in to increase the trespass" (Smalcald Articles III, II, 4-5).

This is the work of God's Law upon both the ungodly and the regenerate, according to Luther. And Melanchthon joins in this judgment in the Apology by saying again and again, *Lex semper accusat* (Apol. IV, 38, 62, 103, 128, 157, 167, 179, 204, 260; XII, 34, 88; cf. Formula of Concord, Solid Declaration I, 6, 31, 32). The Law always accuses, reveals the wrath of God against sin and sinners, condemns the sinner and terrifies him (Apology IV, 38, 131, 144, 257,

260; XII). Luther and Melanchthon are speaking of what Luther calls *passiva contritio*, "true sorrow of the heart, suffering and pain of death"; not the "artificial remorse" (*activa contritio*) of the papists. Luther contended that the papists had watered down sin because in not knowing the true nature of original sin and its consequences they did not really understand what sin is. As a result, they also watered down repentance, teaching and practicing a false repentance whereby the poor sinner had to confess all his mortal sins to the priest before he could receive pardon. The sinner was taught that the purer and more complete his confession, the better he could make satisfaction and earn "grace before God." This practice which ignored faith and Christ bred uncertainty. Luther's description of this practice was that the sinner was "always doing penance, but never coming to repentance" (Smalcald Articles III, 23). In opposition to this "partial and fragmentary" repentance over "actual sins" Luther pointed to the true repentance preached by John the Baptist and the apostles. Luther stated that this true repentance "does not debate what is sin and what is not sin, but lumps everything together and says, 'We are wholly and altogether sinful'" (Smalcald Articles III, III, 36).[27]

Thus, Luther, in a nutshell, described the Lutheran doctrine of sin and repentance. Hereby Luther also marked the real *status controversiae* between the Lutheran position on repentance and the Roman Catholic doctrine and practice of penance. The Lutheran position was that sin totally pervades man's nature and thoroughly corrupts his thoughts, words, and deeds.

True repentance (*die rechte Busse*), too, is never partial, eclectic, or piecemeal, but *total*. In true repentance the sinner confesses to God and repents not only of the sins he has committed (mortal sins, venial sins, sins of omission and sins of commission, remembered sins and forgotten sins, capital sins, and sins of ignorance), but confesses and repents first and foremost of what he is, a poor helpless and lost sinner (Luke 18:13; Psalm 51:5; Smalcald Articles III, III, 37, passim). For every sinner is not only totally sinful, but totally guilty before God, guilty because of his corrupt nature and also guilty because God has declared all men to be guilty (Romans 5:12-21).

Just as one cannot teach correctly about repentance unless one knows what sin really is (Smalcald Articles III, III, 10), so one cannot teach correctly the Gospel of forgiveness and appreciate its comfort (Apology XII, 60; Augsburg Confession XX, 15) unless one acknowledges the magnitude of one's sin. "Recognition of original sin is a necessity, nor can we know the magnitude of the grace of Christ unless we acknowledge our faults. All the righteousness of man is mere hypocrisy before God unless we acknowledge that of itself the heart is lacking in love, fear, and trust in God." (Apology II, 33). Again Melanchthon says, "Christ was given to us to bear both sin and penalty and to destroy the rule of the devil, sin, and death; so we cannot know His blessing unless we recognize our evil" (Apology II, 50).[28]

# Eight

# Grace

The Roman Catholic doctrine of grace has been drawn primarily from the writings of St. Augustine and the medieval scholastic theologians. The doctrine has become increasingly complex over time. The concept of grace was taken up by the scholastic theologians and by modern Roman Catholic dogmaticians after their discussions of Christology. The result was that the doctrine of grace came to be dissociated from Christ's great acts of redemption and reconciliation and became related to the work of the Holy Spirit in the believer's sanctification, that is to say, the theology of the Third Article. The atoning work of Christ became a meritorious cause of grace which made grace possible. The relationship between the work of Christ and the grace of God remained pretty much separated.

What, then, was the grace of God? The medieval scholastic theologians who developed the doctrine and the Roman Catholic opponents of Luther gave scant attention to the biblical data pertaining to the subject. Following St. Augustine, they simply assumed that God's grace, or graces, were God's gifts of grace, freely given (*gratis data*) of His benevolence to rational creatures.[29] By consistently understanding and using the term grace metonymically, they begged the question as to what the grace of God in Christ really was.

All graces, or gifts of grace, were understood to be "actual existing realities."[30] The graces were classified as actual grace and habitual grace.[31] Habitual grace can be defined as the indwelling of the Holy Spirit and the Trinity accompanied by the gift of a *supernatural quality* by which we are made partakers of the divine nature, what the new *Catechism of the Catholic Church* (hereafter *Catholic Catechism*)[32] calls "sanctifying and deifying grace." This supernatural quality was received in Baptism.

Habitual grace contains three elements: 1) An *entitative quality* or *habitus* (propensity, disposition), permanently *inherent* in the soul. Through this quality, or *habitus*, which is *infused* into the soul we become partakers of the divine nature. The infused *habitus* perfects the soul and enables it to act divinely. 2) Infused virtues (faith, hope, love, etc.) are joined to "infused grace." These virtues are existent and have the power, but not the facility, to elicit supernatural acts. They are all received at the moment of justification, which is the beginning of the sanctification process. The infused virtues can be strengthened by the means of grace. 3) Certain gifts of the Holy Spirit which are existent, such as understanding, wisdom, knowledge, counsel (which are intellectual gifts), and piety, fortitude, and fear of God (which are volitional gifts).

*Actual* grace is a passing, supernatural help, or intervention, of God over against the intellect and will of man, enlightening the intellect and empowering the will. There are various kinds of actual grace(s): 1) *gratia operans* and *cooperans*; 2) prevenient grace which precedes a free act, and consequent grace which supports a free activity; 3) *gratia excitans* which moves a salutary work, and *gratia adjuvans* which helps a person to perform a free work; and 4) *gratia medicinalis* which heals and *gratia elevans* which bestows power.

This very brief summary of the elaborate Roman Catholic doctrine of grace represents the *publica doctrina* of Rome, *in rebus et phrasibus*, at least until Vatican II. It is worth noting that Roman Catholic literature (*Catholic Catechism*) and the Lutheran/Roman Catholic dialogue documents (*Joint Declaration*) appearing after Vatican II refrain from much of the older intricate jargon which expressed the traditional Roman Catholic doctrine. For instance, the infusion of grace is not mentioned. But nothing in the pattern of the old doctrine has been compromised or displaced. The doctrine itself remains fully intact.

Luther broke with the scholastic doctrine of grace and its consistent metonymical understanding of the concept (effect for cause). He saw God's grace as related first and foremost to the salvation and justification of a sinner for Christ's sake. He pointedly distinguished between grace and the gifts of grace. He rejected the notion of infused grace, as worked out by the scholastic theologians, often in a synergistic or pelagian context, although into mid-career he used the metaphor of an infusion of grace and of righteousness.[33] After all, the metaphors of pouring (being poured and fullness) are common in Scripture in a variety of contexts (Ephesians 3:19, 5:18; Titus 3:6;

Acts 9:17, 13:9; Romans 5:5; John 1:16), but the metaphors have to do with theological and spiritual realities and divine actions, not with philosophical, metaphysical, or physical referents.

How do Luther and the other reformers demetaphorize the common ecclesiastical term "infuse" and the biblical terms "pour" ("in" or "out") and "fill"? Ordinarily these metaphorical terms mean simply to "give" or to "apply." For instance, the Lutherans at times spoke epexegetically of God pouring out a gift, meaning thereby simply that God gives a gift (Formula of Concord, Solid Declaration II, 48),[34] or bestows His love and blessings. So when Luther and the confessors speak of God giving His grace (Smalcald Articles III, VIII, 3; Small Catechism IV, 9, 12; Large Catechism I, 175; Formula of Concord, Solid Declaration XI, 33, 72), they are referring not to an infusion of a quality which henceforth resides in man but to a mighty, free, loving, giving act of God whereby He elects us in Christ, justifies, and forgives us for Christ's sake, blesses, sanctifies, and saves us—and all that freely given out of His grace in Christ.

What Luther and Melanchthon, in the Apology, objected to most strenuously in the Roman teaching was that grace was considered a "*quality*," or essence, given the believer along with other "finite gifts" and qualities, a quality with which a believer cooperates to obtain more grace. Luther objected more to the non-metaphorical term "*qualitas*" than to the metaphorical term "*infusio*" used by the papists in a non-metaphorical sense, namely, as an *actus physicus*. Luther describes disdainfully the Roman doctrine of grace: "The Sophists . . . teach that grace is a quality which is hidden in the heart. Now if someone has this enclosed in his heart like a jewel, then God will look favorably on him, if he will cooperate with his free will." Luther maintains that the papists distort the biblical and evangelical doctrine of grace when they treat the grace of God, which can only be predicated of God, as a quality among other qualities, human affections and dispositions (*habitus*), such as hope, fortitude, faith, etc. One can refer with good theological and biblical warrant to a believer's faith, hope, and love (the "theological virtues"),[35] but not to a believer's grace. Luther maintains that by teaching that grace is a spiritual quality in man the papists have imposed an alien metaphysics upon the scriptural doctrine of grace, thus resulting in unbearable confusion.[36] The consequence is that righteousness and holiness are thought of as qualities of the soul "smeared and poured" into it, like a color in bread or fur or on a wall,[37] and man in the end is justified and saved by such a quality in man.

However, if the grace of God is not a composite of gifts of grace, and if it is not a composite of infused qualities and virtues, what is it? What is the grace of God according to Lutheran theology? Is it to be classified as a divine attribute, a divine action, or a disposition of God? In a formal sense the grace of God may be considered to fall under all three such classifications. But to classify a concept does not yet tell us what it is.

When Luther and the Lutheran reformers speak of God's grace and explain its meaning, they are not attempting merely to classify it, although the classification definitely enters into the picture. Neither are they engaging merely in onomastics and offering the results of a word or concept study, like modern lexicographers. They are, rather, describing how the term or concept is used in a definite context, a context of the act of God justifying the sinner for Christ's sake and saving him. They are not offering a resumé of the numerous meanings and connotations of the word *charis* and the nuances of the word in the New Testament. Rather, they are establishing what the grace of God is and what the grace of God means in a Christological and soteriological context. This procedure is a legitimate one; the medieval scholastics and Roman Catholic theologians carried out the same procedure.

When Luther and the Lutheran reformers (Melanchthon, Chemnitz, et al.) articulated their doctrine of grace, they were dealing not so much with a vocable, or term, as a concept, a concept called grace and classified and summarized by that term. But the concept was also expressed throughout the Scriptures by many other terms and related concepts such as "mercy," "kindness," "benevolence," and especially "love." Contextualizing the concept within the framework of the work of Christ and soteriology (justification), Luther and the reformers present the grace of God as God's favor—His benevolent and good disposition and intention toward fallen mankind (Titus 2:11; 2 Timothy 1:9). Grace is more than a mere quiescent intention, however. Grace is active; it is in action as God demonstrates His love and grace in sending His Son (Romans 5:8; John 3:16-17) to save sinners (Ephesians 2:8-9; Titus 3:5), to justify them (Galatians 2:16-20;

Romans 3-5), to call, enlighten, convert, and sanctify His children (1 Peter 5:10; John 1:14, 16; Galatians 2:21), and thus create and sustain Christ's Church with gifts of grace [*charismata*] (Romans 12:6; Ephesians 4:7).

In Lutheran theology it is by grace that God sends and gives His Son to be our Savior. Contrariwise, it is the atonement of Christ which propitiates God who is angry with sinners and moves Him to become gracious "for Christ's sake" (Apology XV, 11, 12; IV, 292, 382, 386; Augsburg Confession XXII, 9). In this way we are justified and receive the forgiveness of sins and reconciliation by faith "for Christ's sake" (Apology IV, 159, 163; Augsburg Confession XII, 5). All God's grace is centered in Christ and His atoning work (the theology of the cross). All the gracious actions and blessings and gifts of God are, according to Melanchthon's phrase, *propter Christum*. The Lutheran churches sing, "Jesus, in Thy cross are centered all the marvels of Thy grace."[38] That is no exaggeration. The word grace is given a new meaning in the Sacred Scriptures. It is inextricably conjoined with God's saving work in Christ and in God's giving of His Son. Apart from Christ and His redemption there is no grace, no gracious God.

In Lutheran theology the topic of God's grace is usually considered, like Law and Gospel, early in the locus on justification. It is after, or perhaps in, his discovery of the righteousness of faith that Luther discovered the meaning of the grace of God. The right understanding and doctrine of justification involves the right understanding and doctrine of the grace of God and vise versa.

At the time of the Reformation, Luther, Melanchthon, and the other Lutheran teachers assumed, like their adversaries, the correctness of their own understanding of what God's grace was. It was not until the time of Chemnitz that the meaning of the term and concept was discussed at some length. It was also at this time, after the Council of Trent and the Osiandrian controversy, that concerns centering in the universality of grace and the *sola gratia* became more acute. In his *Examination of the Council of Trent*[39] Chemnitz discusses the term "grace" on the basis of Scripture. The term, he points out, often means favor, benevolence, mercy, and love. Also, at times it means a gift conferred by grace. But his present concern is the meaning of the term in its soteriological context. In this context the term cannot be taken metonymically but means the mercy, goodness, and benevolence by which God justifies the sinner. When Paul in Romans 5 says we are justified and saved by grace, he is referring not to our new life (which is a gift of grace), but to the gratuitous mercy of God who justifies us only for Christ's sake. Here "in the article of justification" grace excludes all works and merit, yet is "in opposition" to them; not only to the "good works" which "reason performs" (what Luther and Melanchthon called *justitia civilis*), but to the works of the regenerate saints (Romans 3:24-28, 4:4). The apostle makes this principle clear, "If it is by grace, it is no longer of works, otherwise grace would no longer be grace" (Romans 11:6; cf. 2 Timothy 1:9). To Chemnitz it is clear that both the meaning and usage of the term in Scripture preclude good works, right attitude, merit, exercise of free will, and anything at all on the part of man as contributing factors in the sinner's justification. Even repentance and faith, which receives the mercy and grace of God, do not merit justification or God's grace, but are the results of His grace. The sinner is justified *sola gratia* for Christ's sake. Grace in the nature of the case is free, *dorean*, not conditioned by anything we do or fail to do or by any preparation we may make for God's grace. Sinners are "justified *freely* by His grace through the redemption which is in Christ Jesus" (Romans 3:24).

The inescapable conclusion to be drawn from these biblical data collected by Chemnitz is that a sinner is justified *sola gratia*. The teaching of justification *sola gratia* became a principle, a watchword, in both doctrine and church life for Lutherans. In worship, preaching, and church life the Gospel of justification by grace alone gives all honor to God and at the same time gives the believer peace of conscience, assurance, and certainty that he is forgiven and saved (Smalcald Articles III, III, 10-45; Apology IV, 148; XII, 88; Formula of Concord, Solid Declaration IV, 9). *Sola gratia* means that the believer did not have to depend on himself in any way, upon what he did or failed to do to prepare for grace and to receive it. Salvation is entirely God's work of grace. *Sola gratia* means that grace is conditioned on nothing in man; and so the Gospel Word and promise, too, by which the Church lives and by which the Church receives the grace of God, is unconditioned.

The principle of *sola gratia* was applied theologically by Lutherans to maintain and defend the correct doctrine of sin, man and free will, the atonement, justification, conversion and regeneration, and, of course, the doctrine of the means of grace. Not to their credit, the later Lutheran dogmaticians (Quenstedt, Hollaz) discussed the concept of grace more thoroughly in the polemical sections of their writings than in the positive sections. To their credit, they brought the subject of grace into their discussions of almost all the soteriological themes, especially those falling within the Third Article of the Creed. Unfortunately, as time went on, they focused less and less direct attention on the topic of grace in their treatment of the high priestly office and saving work of Christ.[40]

By the principle of *sola gratia* the Lutherans not only ruled out all human merit, work righteousness, and synergism in the article of justification, but asserted that Christ's satisfaction was the only satisfaction for men's sin and that it was a perfect (sufficient) and adequate satisfaction to God for the sins of the world. Thus, the sacrifice of the Mass was repudiated, for absolutely nothing can be brought forth to improve or add to Christ's perfect and adequate sacrifice for the sins of the world. The Lord's Supper is not a source of grace but a means of grace, what the Apology calls a "sign of grace," (Apol. XXIV, 69) which not only points us to the one and only perfect sacrifice for sins, but connects and joins us through faith (Apol. XXIV, 72, 92) to that sacrifice which is the source of all grace, forgiveness, and salvation. The doctrine of purgatory is also to be rejected as being in conflict with the *sola gratia* (Apol. XXIV, 90; X, 118, 123; Smalcald Articles II, II, 13, 14). *Sola gratia* dispels doubt; purgatory creates doubt (Smalcald Articles II, II, 21-27).

It was not only with Rome that the Lutherans differed on the doctrine of grace. Against the Calvinistic doctrine of predestination the Lutherans asserted that God's grace extends equally to all, that Christ's work of atonement is universal, and that the Gospel and grace of God are to be preached and offered to all seriously and without discrimination (Formula of Concord, Solid Declaration XI, 14-23). God earnestly desires to save all and to consign no one to hell. Trent (Session VI, Canon 17) agreed on this last point, and Rome agreed that Christ's atonement extended to all. But the doctrine of habitual grace conflicted with universal grace according to the confessional Lutherans, for habitual grace was not equally dispensed by God to all (Trent, Session VI, Chapter VII). This disagreement can only be overcome when grace is seen as a disposition in God rather than as a gift in man.

To this day the Lutherans and the Roman Catholics have not resolved their differences on the doctrine of grace. For over four centuries they have polemicized and debated and, more recently, dialogued, each side using its own distinctive meaning of the term. This approach has resulted in ambiguity. If there is verbal agreement that salvation is by grace, and the two sides mean something different by the term "grace," then their doctrine of salvation will be different; and the ambiguity is compounded. If the two sides mean something different by the term "salvation," then the ambiguity is compounded still further. Fruitful and meaningful discourse for the purpose of reaching doctrinal consensus cannot take place, especially after centuries of disagreement and misunderstanding, unless there is clear and careful agreement on the meaning of all terms essential to the discourse. If such ground rules are not accepted by both sides and applied, the result will be analogous to two Mormons visiting a Christian home and telling the Catholic or Lutheran families to whom they speak, "We are Christians. We believe in the Triune God."

Unfortunately, just such a development seems to have taken place in all the recent dialogues between Lutherans and Roman Catholics on the subject of grace. Each side has come to the conference table with its own distinctive and firm understanding of what the grace of God is, and a convergence or consensus statement has been worked out which ignores the fact that both sides completely disagree on what the grace of God is.

In fact, there has been precious little discussion of the concept of grace in any of the studies and documents emanating from recent Roman Catholic/Lutheran dialogue on the doctrine of justification. Both Roman Catholics and Lutherans emphatically teach in their respective confessions that justification takes place by the grace of God. However, both the Lutheran doctrine that justification by grace is a declaration of total acquittal and the Roman Catholic doctrine that justification by God's grace is a transformation, or "change wrought in the sinner by infused grace,"[41] are recognized as legitimate "images" of what happens when God justifies a sinner. Thus, the utterly divergent Lutheran and Roman Catholic teachings concerning grace are assumed to be merely elements of a particular image "of conceptualizing or picturing God's saving work." And recognition of this fact represents, according to *Justification by Faith*, a "material convergence" which has now been discovered or achieved.[42]

*Condemnations of the Reformation Era* does no more to address the dispute on the nature of grace than *Justification by Faith*. Like *Justification by Faith* and *On Justification*, *Condemnations of the Reformation Era* makes much of the contributions of modern biblical studies and historical research in Roman Catholic and Lutheran discussions, particularly in bringing to light the great problem of equivocation which marked and impeded all interconfessional discussion until recently. *Condemnations of the Reformation Era* rightly points out that such ambiguity in the use of key terms relative to the doctrine of justification and the inability or unwillingness of both sides to establish any ground rules or agreement in the definition and use of the terms resulted in misunderstanding, unfair and exaggerated polemics, and distortions of their party's position. This was indeed tragic.

However, *Condemnations of the Reformation Era* draws an erroneous conclusion from that sad state of affairs. The conclusion drawn is that the different contents and meanings attached to the terms and concepts relative to the doctrine of justification were merely battles over words, different interpretative stresses, different concerns and emphases, relevant and perhaps valid in that bygone day but not in ours. Modern ecumenical discussions have changed that previous state of affairs. According to *Condemnations of the Reformation Era* these discussions have cleared up much misunderstanding, brought about openness and appreciation to other traditions and insights, and revealed the startling discovery that what were formerly real doctrinal controversies are no longer so. Hence, the foregone conclusion that the condemnations proceeding from Trent and the Lutheran Confessions are no longer applicable. Thus, there is no longer a compelling reason for clearing up the ambiguity between the Roman Catholic and Lutheran understandings of what the grace of God is, no need to establish a common understanding of what the grace of God is as an activity in God's order of salvation, no need to discuss the doctrine of grace per se or whether there is a *doctrine* of grace at all. Perhaps this judgment seems severe, but it is warranted.[43] *Condemnations of the Reformation Era* even suggests that the doctrine of grace taught in the Reformation Era was not very far from the scholastic doctrine of Rome (51); this on the slender evidence that Melanchthon on one occasion in the Apology (IV, 116) uses the scholastic term *gratia gratum faciens* (grace that makes us acceptable to God), a technical term which refers to what the scholastic theologians called sanctifying grace. Such an allegation is grasping at straws. There is no evidence that Melanchthon, who used the word grace more than a hundred times in the Augsburg Confession and the Apology, ever had in mind the Roman doctrine of infused grace.

*Joint Declaration* accepts the conclusion of *Justification by Faith* and *Condemnations of the Reformation Era* and sets the Lutheran *understanding* of grace as God's forgiving love alongside the Roman Catholic *emphasis* on the life-renewing power of grace (*gratia habitualis*) to impart a gift of active love (man's love). Then *Joint Declaration* simply proclaims consensus. To this glib conclusion we must respond as follows. First, can one person's understanding of an object and another person's emphasis upon an aspect of that same object represent meaningful consensus? More importantly, when two parties say they depend upon the saving grace of God for salvation, and by grace one party means the saving, loving disposition of God and the other party means an infused quality, can they both be said to share a common confession?

A fundamental question seems not to have been asked in any of the extensive dialogues. The question is: What is the biblical doctrine of grace? Why is this question not addressed? It is probable that to ask this question seriously would be to threaten the entire Roman Catholic doctrine of grace, which is based upon St. Augustine's notion of *gratia data* and *gratia creata*. Roman Catholic participants in the various dialogues simply could not allow their ecclesiastical doctrine of grace to be examined critically in the light of Scripture. *Gratia infusa* and *gratia habitualis* have no basis in Scripture.[44]

# Nine

# Justification, *Propter Christum*, and the Imputation of Christ's Righteousness

T he sinner is justified by grace for Christ's sake through faith."
After the terms "sin" and "grace," the third key word in the classic formulation of Luther's doctrine of justification is the word "justify." The entire doctrine of justification hinges on the meaning of that key word. What does it mean to be justified? What is the nature of God's justification of the sinner?

The most important treatment of justification by faith written by any of the Lutheran reformers was Article IV of Melanchthon's Apology of the Augsburg Confession. Luther's more spirited discussion in the Smalcald Articles and in his *Galatians Commentary* and in many other writings may have made more overall impact upon Lutherans and other Protestants, but Apology IV, written just one year after the Augsburg Confession, gave the Lutheran doctrine a symbolic status and set the tone for all future dogmatic and confessional treatments of the chief article and its many adjunct articles (Formula of Concord III, IV, V, VI). Apology IV puts the article of justification in its proper setting, i.e., between Article II on original sin and Article V in the Augsburg Confession on the ministry of the Word and Sacrament, and Article VI on the new obedience and the later articles on the Church, Baptism, the Lord's Supper, etc. Within Apology IV Melanchthon treats justification in relation to the preaching of Law and Gospel, the means of grace, and the new obedience of the justified sinner. He also deals with the biblical terminology and topics which are an integral part of the doctrine, such as: the grace of God, the righteousness of faith, the righteousness of Christ, and faith.[45] It is, therefore, imperative that we examine the theology of Apology IV on the article of justification.

Melanchthon defines the verb "to justify" as denoting a forensic act, and his entire treatment of justification issues from this conception and is dependent upon it. Melanchthon's definition of the word "justify" is found in a comment on the use of the word in Romans 5:1 (Apology IV, 305): "In this passage the word 'justify' is used in a judicial way to mean 'to absolve a guilty man and pronounce him righteous,' and to do so on account of someone else's righteousness, namely, Christ's, which is communicated to us through faith." Throughout the Apology and the other confessions the term is consistently understood and used in this sense.[46]

At times Melanchthon speaks of regeneration as a part of what happens when a person is justified. He is not thereby adding regeneration, spiritual rebirth, to his definition of justification, but referring to a concomitant to the event of justification. When a person is justified by faith he is also regenerated. "Therefore we are justified by faith alone, justification being understood as making an unregenerate man righteous or effecting his regeneration" (Apology IV, 78). In another place Melanchthon says (Apology IV, 72), "and to be 'justified' means to make unrighteous men righteous or to regenerate them, as well as to be pronounced or accounted righteous." The moment faith is brought into the picture of a sinner's justification before God, regeneration is brought into the picture, too; for regeneration is the gift of faith. Justification by faith *involves* regeneration to faith (cf. Apology IV, 117). Apparently, some confusion developed over Melanchthon's linking justification to regeneration so closely. The Formula of Concord (Solid Declaration III, 19) cleared up this difficulty:

> Since the word "regeneration" is used in place of "justification," it is necessary to explain the term strictly so that the renewal which follows justification by faith will not be confused with justification and so that in their strict senses the two will be differentiated from each other. The word "regeneration" is used, in the first place, to include "the forgiveness of sins solely for Christ's sake and the consequent renewal which the Holy Spirit works in those who are justified by faith." But this word is also used in the limited sense of the forgiveness of sins and our adoption as God's children. In this latter sense it is frequently used in the Apology, where the statement is made, "justification is regeneration," that is, justification before God is regeneration, just as St. Paul uses the terms discriminately when he states, "He saved us by the washing of regeneration and renewing of the Holy Spirit" (Titus 3:5).

In this same sense Luther and all the later Lutheran theologians to this day have used the word. According to this definition, based upon its usage in Scripture, the word means to declare a sinner righteous and to impute Christ's righteousness to him. This definition of the meaning of the word includes a formal definition of what God's action in justifying a sinner is. This formal definition of the nature of justification, of what God's act of justification is, is followed by all the confessional Lutheran theologians after the Reformation and is essential to their presentation of the doctrine of justification by faith. Responding to the aberrations of Andrew Osiander and Trent, the Formula of Concord returns to this basic understanding of what the term "justification" means and what justification is (Solid Declaration III, 17):

> Accordingly the word "justify" here means to declare righteous and free from sins and from the eternal punishment of these sins on account of the righteousness of Christ which God reckons to faith (Philippians 3:9). And this is the usual usage and meaning of the word in the Holy Scriptures of the Old and New Testaments.

As time went on the *definitions of justification* became more complete, elaborate, and material in content, and included a description, sometimes quite detailed, of the bases and "causes" of justification as well as what happens when a sinner is justified. A typical example of this procedure can be found in Balthasar Mentzer's *Exegesis of the Augsburg Confession*:

> Justification is an act of God the Father, God the Son, and Holy Spirit, an act which forgives the sinner all his sins, imputes to him the righteousness of Christ and receives him into everlasting life. It is an act of pure grace, love and mercy, performed because of the most perfect obedience which our Mediator Christ rendered to the entire divine Law and because of the full satisfaction He made. The sinner is justified who through the ministry of the Gospel truly believes that Christ is the Redeemer of the whole world, and he is justified by grace without his own works or merits.[47]

It is notable that Mentzer in this statement includes all the aforementioned key terms and parts of the article of justification: sin, grace, faith, and Christ's work of atonement, as well as the imputation of Christ's righteousness, the ministry of the Gospel, and the goal of it all, eternal life. All these themes are woven into a single definition of what justification is.

Chemnitz, in his *Loci Theologici*, offers a much more complete explanation of all that is involved in the forensic doctrine of justification. He draws his lovely description of justification from the forensic meaning of the terms and the forensic nature of the divine act.

> The forensic term indicates that the justification of the sinner is not something trifling or perfunctory; but the whole man stands in the presence of God's judgment, and he is examined according to his nature and his works—and that by the rule of divine Law. However, after sin entered the world, man in this life does not truly and completely conform to the Law of God. Thus nothing can be found in man, either in his nature or his works, which he can offer so that he might be justified before God. Rather the Law pronounces the sentence of condemnation upon him, a sentence written with the finger of God. Now God does not justify the ungodly through some error, like a judge who passes a verdict when he has not examined or acquainted himself sufficiently with the case. Nor does God justify the ungodly carelessly, as though He were not really disturbed over the transgression of His Law. Nor does He justify in an unfair manner, as though He approved of injustice and connived and colluded with the ungodly. God Himself would adjudge such a justification to be an abomination (Exodus 23:1; Isaiah 5:23; Proverbs 17:15). No, God cannot take back His decision of condemnation which is revealed in the Law unless He has been given satisfaction (Matthew 5:18). If God is to justify, justice and satisfaction are required. Luther correctly said, God remits no sin unless justification has been rendered for it to the Law. . . . And so because God does not justify out of fickleness or carelessness or mistakenness or injustice and because nothing can be found in man by which he can be justified by God—and yet the righteousness of the Law must be fulfilled in the one to be justified (Romans 8:4)—it is necessary that a foreign righteousness intervene. This foreign righteousness is such that the payment of guilt and the complete obedience of the Law satisfied divine wrath. And the result is that there can be a propitiation for the sins of the whole world. To this righteousness the sinner, terrified and condemned by the voice of the Law, flees with true faith. He desires, implores, and seizes this righteousness. To this righteousness he surrenders himself. This righteousness he sets against the

judgment of God and accusation of the Law. By virtue of this righteousness and its being imputed to him he is justified, that is, absolved from the sweeping sentence of condemnation, and he receives the decree of life eternal.[48]

In Lutheran theology justification is seen as having two parts: 1) forgiveness, or the non-imputation of sin, and 2) the imputation of a righteousness outside of us, a foreign or alien righteousness (*justitia aliena*), namely, the righteousness of Christ.

What is this foreign righteousness? It is a righteousness which comes from God (Romans 1:17), but it is not His essential righteousness, not the righteousness by which He judges sinners, nor the righteousness by which He redeems them from their sins. Rather this divine righteousness revealed in the Gospel is the righteousness of His Son Jesus Christ. But again, it is not Christ's essential righteousness, the righteousness of His divine nature. It is rather the righteousness of Christ, the God Man, which He fulfilled and accomplished and acquired for us. It is the saving righteousness (*dikaiosunē*) of His obedience (*dikaiōma, hupokoē*) to the Father (Romans 5:18-19; Philippians 2:8; Hebrews 5:8), His obedience under the Law (Galatians 4:4), by which He obeyed the Law as our Substitute (*huper hēmōn*), and obeyed the will of the Father to die innocently as our Substitute, and thus to redeem us (Galatians 3:13).

This righteousness of Christ, this vicarious obedience under the Law and vicarious obedience unto death, results in the redemption of the world and the reconciliation of the world to God. This righteousness which constitutes the vicarious atonement is the basis of the sinner's justification before God. But this righteousness also *constitutes* the sinner's justification before God. It is precisely this righteousness which is imputed to the sinner who believes, and thereby becomes his righteousness (Philippians 3:9). It is the purpose of the Formula of Concord (Solid Declaration III, 15-16) to affirm just this fact.

It is this righteousness of Christ, imputed to the believer, that Melanchthon has in mind throughout Apology IV when he speaks of the "righteousness of faith" in contrast to the "righteousness of the Law" or the "righteousness of works."

Luther's discovery of the meaning of "righteousness" in Romans 1:17 was a discovery also of the *justitia aliena* which was at the heart of justification. His discovery of the *justitia aliena* in turn brought Christ and His saving work directly into the article of justification and into his preaching of the Gospel. The result was that for Luther the preaching of the Gospel became in essence the preaching of justification, and the justification of the sinner, the imputation of Christ's righteousness, became the Gospel. In a sermon in 1532 Luther preaches that Gospel:

> The Christian Church is righteous and holy, and yet it does not appear to be so. The reason is this: Christian righteousness is outside us, it is in Christ alone and in faith in Him. Thus, the Christian Church and each Christian confesses and says, I know that I am sinful and unclean, that I lie in prison, in danger, in death, in disgrace and shame, and I feel in myself nothing but sin; and yet I am righteous and holy, not in myself, but in Christ Jesus who of God is made for me wisdom and righteousness and sanctification and redemption.[49]

Again, commenting on John 16:10, Luther says:

> [This righteousness] is not a thought, a word, or work in ourselves, as the scholastics fancied about grace when they said that it is something poured into our heart. No, it is entirely outside and above us; it is Christ's going to the Father, that is, His suffering, resurrection, and ascension. Christ's place is outside the sphere of our senses; we cannot see and feel it. The only way it can be grasped is by faith in the Word preached about Him, which tells us that He Himself is our righteousness. . . .
>
> This is a wonderful righteousness, wonderful indeed that we are called righteous and possess a righteousness which is really no work, no thought, nothing at all in us, but entirely outside of us in Christ. And yet it truly becomes ours through His grace and gift, our very own as though we had acquired and earned it. . . .
>
> Therefore learn this lesson well, that you may be able to distinguish between the righteousness which is of Christ and all else which men call righteousness. For here you learn that the righteousness of which Christ is speaking is not our work or doing, but it is His going to the Father. Now it is clear and obvious that these two kinds of righteousness are foreign to each other. Our work is not Christ, and His going to the Father is not our deed or work. For what have I or anyone else to do with this, that He goes

to the Father, that is, that He suffers and dies and rises again and sits at the right hand of God? This is no obedience or good work of mine but is given by Christ alone and is established in His person.[50]

One of Luther's most trenchant statements concerning the imputed righteousness of Christ is in his 1535 *Commentary on Galatians* (Galatians 2:20) where Luther applies the imputed righteousness of Christ to himself and his own Christian life. I quote him at length.

> Here Christ and my conscience ought to become one body, so that nothing remains before my sight but Christ crucified and raised from the dead. For if I look only in myself and close out Christ I am lost. But then I immediately fall into this way of thinking: Christ is in heaven, you are on earth, how then can you go to Him? It is simple, I will live a holy life and do what the Law demands; then I will enter into life. Thus, turning to myself and looking into myself, into what I am and ought to be and do, I lose sight of Christ who alone is my righteousness and my life. And when He is lost, then there is no counsel, no help, but despair and destruction most certainly follow.

> This is a very common evil. For such is our misery, that in temptation and death, we forget about Christ and consider only our life and deeds. And unless we are raised again by faith we will surely perish. Therefore in such troubles of conscience we must learn to leave ourselves and the Law and all works which only compel us to look to ourselves again, and turn our eyes to that brazen serpent, Christ crucified, who when we cling to Him is our righteousness and our life, and we must not fear the terrors of the Law, or sin, or death, or the wrath or judgment of God.

> Christ and I must be joined together so that He lives in me and I in Him—and what a wonderful way of speaking this is. For because He lives in me, whatever there is in me of grace, righteousness, life, peace, salvation, is all His but in such a way that it is mine through this inseparable union and conjunction which I have with Him through faith. Through this faith Christ and I are made one body, as it were, and spirit. Now because Christ lives in me there must be present with Him grace, righteousness, life, and salvation whereas the Law, sin, and death are absent; in fact, the Law is crucified and devoured and destroyed along with sin, death, and the devil. Thus, Paul tries to draw us wholly away from ourselves and transplant us into Christ by faith in Him, so that in the matter of justification we think of nothing else but grace and separate this from the Law and works which must have no place in this matter.

Paul has his own peculiar way of speech here which is not human but divine and heavenly, and it is not used by the other evangelists and apostles except John who is wont to speak this way once in a while. And if Paul had not spoken this way and set forth this matter in plain words to us, not even the saints would have dared to speak in such a way. For he speaks in an insolent and unheard of manner when he says: "I live, I do not live; I am dead, I am not dead; I am a sinner, I am not a sinner; I have the Law, I haven't the Law." These words are true in Christ and through Christ. But if in this matter of justification you separate the person of Christ from your own person, then you are in the Law and you remain in it and you live in yourself, and then you are dead before God and are damned by the Law. For then you have the faith of which the Sophists prattle, faith furnished with love. I bring this up as an example. For there is no such faith. Therefore what those Sophists teach about faith furnished with love is a mockery of Satan. But let us grant that there are actually men who have such a faith; they are still not saved by it, for it is only a historic faith concerning Christ, something that the devils and all unbelievers also have.

No, we must rightly teach faith, that through faith you are so closely joined together with Christ that you and He are made as one person which can never be separated but always remains united. So you can say, I am as Christ, and Christ in turn says, I am that sinner who holds to Me. For by faith we are so joined together as to become one flesh and bone (Ephesians 5).[51]

Luther brings two closely related motifs together in this statement: 1) Christ's imputed righteousness, and 2) Christ's "blessed exchange" with us whereby "He took upon Himself our personal sins and gave to us His personal innocence and victory."[52] How do we coordinate these two motifs in Luther's theology? Elsewhere, as we have seen, he asserts that a believer has the righteousness of Christ (*justitia aliena*) on the basis of God's imputation. Here it might appear that the believer possesses Christ's righteousness by being united with Christ through faith. Do we explain this seeming discrepancy by noting that here is an example of Luther's "sitting loose on vocabulary," or freely engaging in "dialectical contrasts," or passing "from one problematic to another despite differences in language and perspectives," a tendency in Luther correctly observed by George Tavard?[53] In other words, is Luther inconsistent or just sloppy? Perhaps he is just mixing "metaphors" at this point. Such an explanation is, of course, possible but highly unlikely.

The Formula of Concord gives Luther's doctrine of the imputed *justitia aliena* symbolical status and describes carefully what the imputed righteousness of Christ is.

> Therefore the righteousness which by grace is reckoned to faith or to the believers is obedience, the passion, and the resurrection of Christ when He satisfied the Law for us and paid for our sin. Since Christ is not only man, but God and man in one undivided person, He was as little under the Law—since He is the Lord of the Law—as He was obligated to suffer and die for His person. Therefore His obedience consists not only in His suffering and dying, but also in His spontaneous subjection to the Law in our stead and His keeping of the Law in so perfect a fashion that, reckoning it to us as righteousness, God forgives us our sins, accounts us holy and righteous, and saves us forever on account of this entire obedience which, by doing and suffering, in life and in death, Christ rendered for us to His heavenly Father. This righteousness is offered to us by the Holy Spirit through the Gospel and in the Sacraments, and is applied, appropriated, and accepted by faith, so that thus believers have reconciliation with God, forgiveness of sins, and the grace of God, adoption, and the inheritance of eternal life. (Solid Declaration III, 14-16)

The imputation of Christ's righteousness to the believer is not a metaphorical motif to Luther but a non-figurative description of what actually takes place when a sinner is justified for Christ's sake. And there is no other way in which a sinner can be justified and become righteous before God except by the imputation of Christ's righteousness. Furthermore, the setting for the imputation of Christ's righteousness to the believer is not figurative. Sin, God's judgment, grace, redemption, Christ's obedience and life and death are not figures of speech. The "blessed exchange" motif, however, while not metaphorical in itself, is set in a metaphorical pattern of thought (marriage, union with Christ, crucifixion of Law, sin, and death, etc.). Therefore we can conclude that Luther is not mixing metaphors or confusing two motifs at all. Rather, he is grounding the blessed exchange whereby the believer receives forgiveness and spiritual blessings from Christ and Christ in turn receives the sinner's sin and guilt and punishment in the fact of the believer's justification before God for Christ's sake. In other words, God for Christ's sake imputes to the believer Christ's righteousness and imputes to Christ the believer's sin and guilt. This is how the blessed exchange takes place. It is not possible to understand Luther as grounding the blessed exchange in the fact of the believer's union with Christ. To do so would deny that the *justitia aliena* is imputed and would put the two motifs in opposition to each other. Furthermore, union with Christ is the result of justification, not the other way around.

The coordination and agreement of the two motifs is easily perceived when we observe that Luther (whose exegesis included interpretation and application) is not interpreting Galatians 2:20 in the above citation, but rather applying the apostle's very personal testimony at this point. One who is justified by grace is at the same time united with Christ. This means that the believer continually applies the blessed exchange and the *justitia aliena* to himself.

The doctrine of imputed righteousness is simply repudiated by Rome (Trent, Ses. VI, canon 10). The doctrine does not fit Rome's doctrine of infused grace, infused righteousness, and infused faith. As a matter of fact, it is at this point that the chasm between Luther's "Christocentric"[54] doctrine of justification and the Roman doctrine becomes most apparent. Rome did not, however, discard the righteousness of Christ as playing no role in our justification. Neither did Rome reject or object to the term "impute," which was a very common term in the vocabulary of scholastic theology.[55] What Rome rejected was the joining of the two concepts. Rome rejected the doctrine that the imputation of Christ's righteousness or the merit of Christ, and nothing else, constitutes justification, the sinner's righteousness before God.

In this context Trent's canon condemning the Lutheran doctrine needs to be examined. The canon reads as follows: "If anyone says that men are justified without the righteousness of Christ whereby He has merited for us, or that through this righteousness we become righteous formally (*formaliter*), let him be anathema." Although condemnatory in form, the canon makes two correlative assertions about justification which were fundamental to the Roman Catholic doctrine of justification—and still are.

First, the "righteousness of Christ," the merits of Christ (referring to Christ's passion and propitiatory death), is according to Trent the meritorious cause, the *causa meritoria* (Trent, Ses. VI, chap. 8) of justification. Essentially, that means that Christ's atoning work makes justification and sanctification by grace possible. Second, the righteousness of Christ's doing and suffering is not the righteousness by which we become righteous. The righteousness of Christ's doing and suffering is not imputed to us in justification at all. It has nothing to do with the nature (*forma*) of our righteousness before God. The nature of our justification, what constitutes our righteousness before God and makes this righteousness what it is, the "single formal cause" (*unica causa formalis*) is not the imputed obedience and righteousness of Christ. Rather, it is "the righteousness of God, not that by which He Himself is righteous, but that by which He makes us righteous (*nos justos facit*), namely, that with which we being endowed by Him and are renewed in the spirit of our mind (Ephesians 4:23). Not only are we reputed (*reputamus*) but we are truly called and are righteous, receiving righteousness within us (*in nobis*), each according to his own measure which the Holy Spirit distributes to everyone as He wills, and according to each one's disposition and cooperation" (Trent, Ses. VI, chap. 7).[56]

The upshot of this Roman Catholic two-pronged conception of the relation of the righteousness (merit) of Christ and the sinner's justification is the divorce of any real, formal connection between Christ's work of redemption and the sinner's justification. The redemptive work of Christ is relegated exclusively to the theology of the Second Article and the doctrine of grace, sanctification and justification to the Third Article. Luther's "Christocentric" theology of justification (Smalcald Articles II, II, 1 ff.) is effectively jettisoned.

Although Luther's and the confessional view of the imputed *justitia aliena* was derived directly from the Scriptures, it was unknown to the scholastic theology preceding the Reformation. Thus, Roman Catholic theologians of Luther's day, enmeshed in scholastic theology, were incapable of giving the Lutheran doctrine a hearing. They perceived that the doctrine of imputed righteousness was an attack on the Roman doctrine of grace—which it was—so they dug in their heels.

The basic argument against the *justitia imputata* of Christ was against the propriety of the doctrine. Trent followed the scholastic theology, exemplified by Bonaventure,[57] who taught that "neither to the resurrection nor passion [of Christ] can be attributed properly (*proprie*) the causality of justification or the remission of guilt," since justification is in a different category (*modo*) from Christ's passion and resurrection. It is obvious that Bonaventure did not consider the active obedience of Christ (Romans 5:15), His obedience to the Law and under the Law (which is clearly commensurate with man's disobedience to the Law), as a part of His righteousness and atonement. The scholastics made little of the active obedience of Christ as a part of Christ's atoning work, and they restricted the merits of Christ to His death (Anselm; so also the *Catholic Catechism*, 1992). Trent simply and uncritically followed scholastic theology at this point, making the righteousness of Christ a remote meritorious cause of justification and thus detaching it from justification itself.

Chemnitz in his *Examination of the Council of Trent* addresses this crucial issue and defines Rome's position as follows: "Through its interpreter Andrada the Council of Trent declares publicly that Christ merited for us only the infusion of love in order that by the power of His love which dwells in us sins might be driven out and destroyed."[58]

In addition to the argument against the propriety of the *justitia imputata*, two other significant objections were advanced by Rome against the doctrine of imputed righteousness. First, the Romanists argued that a verdict of God which imputed Christ's righteousness to the sinner has no foundation. To this objection of Jacob Andrada, the Jesuit commentator on the Council of Trent, Chemnitz responds that God indeed does not pass verdicts without a basis (*fundamentum*); such a verdict would be an abomination (Deuteronomy 25:1; Proverbs 17:15; Isaiah 5:20, 23). The verdict, however, whereby God declares the sinner righteous does not have its foundation in the believer in any sense, in his works, his infused virtues, or any activity wrought in him by grace. The foundation of the imputation is outside of him entirely, in Christ "our Mediator who was made under the Law and made satisfaction to the Law by carrying our sins and obeying the Law perfectly."[59] Thus, Chemnitz concludes, "We have a true verdict and it is based on the obedience and redemption of Christ."

At this point it becomes evident that there is complete equivocation between Trent and the theologians of the Formula of Concord on the meaning of the key phrase *propter Christum.* Trent said, "It is necessary to believe that sins neither are remitted nor ever have been remitted except gratuitously by divine mercy *for Christ's sake*" (Trent, Ses. VI, chap. 9). Time and again Melanchthon in the Apology makes statements like the following: "We are accounted righteous before God *for Christ's sake* by faith" (Apology IV, 214). "The forgiveness of sins is granted us freely *for Christ's sake*" (Apology XI, 2). "By faith we freely obtain the forgiveness of sins *for Christ's sake*" (Apology XXVIII, 23). "We receive forgiveness of sins and become righteous before God by grace *for Christ's sake,* through faith" (Augsburg Confession IV, 2). However, Melanchthon and Trent, while both using the phrase *propter Christum,* are worlds apart in the meaning they give the phrase. Melanchthon and the Lutheran Confessions mean that the righteousness of Christ was the basis, the source, the cause, and the essence (*forma*) of the sinner's righteousness before God. Trent and its spokesmen to this very day, including the *Catholic Catechism,* mean only that Christ by His atoning death created a situation in which God can justify and sanctify a person through his own virtues infused into him by grace.

Modern dialogues conducted by Roman Catholics and Lutherans have used the *propter Christum,* so dear to the Lutheran heart, sparingly, if at all. And there seems to be little attempt to establish any consensus on the meaning of the phrase or to attach an unequivocal meaning to it. Perhaps the participants in the various dialogues failed to see that the meaning of the phrase *propter Christum* was a clear point of controversy in the sixteenth century.

*Joint Declaration* seems to be aware of the difference, however, when it says that to Lutherans the saving act of Christ is the basis of justification, and then contrasts this position to the Roman Catholic view that sinners are made righteous through sanctifying grace, a view which ignores Christ's atonement and righteousness as having any direct part in the actual justification of a sinner. At this point *Joint Declaration* lets the matter drop. Apparently it is not very important that Lutherans believe that the saving act of Christ is the basis of our justification and Rome does not.

The second Roman Catholic criticism of the *justitia aliena* imputed to us in justification lay in the Catholic claim that justification consisted of more than a bare imputation and forgiveness. More happens in justification. Present also are the Holy Spirit, regeneration, hope, charity, and sanctification. Rome did not dispute that there was a divine imputation involved in the sinner's justification before God. And as time went on Rome did not seriously dispute that the word *dikaioō* was a forensic term. The massive evidence for this fact brought forth by Chemnitz and the later Lutherans was utterly compelling.[60] Roman Catholic theology simply broadened the idea of justification, according to an etymological understanding of the Latin word "*justificatio*" (make righteous), to denote a process of becoming gradually more righteous. Justification was a change (*mutatio*) in a person, an improvement. Cardinal Robert Bellarmine expressed the Roman Catholic teaching as follows: "Ordinarily a person is said to be warmed not only when from being cold he is made warm, but when from being warm he is made warmer. So too one is said to be justified not only when from being unrighteous he is made righteous, but when from being righteous he is made more righteous."[61] The process of justification was also likened to the model of getting well: Christ was considered the Great Physician (Matthew 9:12) who heals us and strengthens us. But we get well gradually through the infusion of grace (*gratia medicinalis, sanans*).[62] Thus, justification is viewed as a "physical and medicinal action" whereby the unrighteous man is changed by an inward transformation into a righteous one.

By defining the nature (*forma in genere*) of justification as a process, Roman Catholic theology in effect denied that justification was by nature a divine reckoning or forensic act.[63] *In genere* justification is *either* God's acquittal and declaration that the sinner is for Christ's sake righteous, a declaration which takes place outside man, *or* justification is a moral change, or process, which consists in the sinner "obtaining" an "inherent righteousness," or, to put it differently, the sinner's "acquisition of an infused *habitus* of righteousness."[64] Both Roman Catholic theology and Lutheran theology were well aware of this. The two differing views on the nature of justification were mutually exclusive.

The Lutherans were able in good conscience to call justification a "change," but only in the sense of a change of status, not an inner change, or process, taking place in the sinner.[65] The believer is no longer under the wrath of God. Being justified by faith, he *has* peace with God through Christ (Romans 5:1). His status before God and relationship to God have been completely changed. He is in a state of grace; no longer a sinner before God but righteous before God. David Hollaz says, "By the benefit of justification the sinner is changed *extrinsically*, in the sense of a change in status. This means that the sinner, who is under the absolute righteous judgment of God but has also been reconciled through Christ, is transferred from a state of sin and wrath to a state of grace and righteousness."[66]

The Lutherans were also concerned to affirm that when a sinner is justified, other things happen as well. They happen in the sinner, and they always happen. The justified sinner is born again (regeneration is the gift of faith, Galatians 3:26-27) and becomes an heir of salvation. He receives the Holy Spirit who sanctifies him with His gifts (Word and Sacraments, ministers of the Word, continuous forgiveness, comfort, etc.). He is united with Christ and the Holy Trinity in the most intimate *unio mystica*; he is also empowered by the Holy Spirit, working in the Word, to do good works which please God, not for their own sake—for they are always tainted with sin—but for Christ's sake, because the believer is God's child who belongs to Christ, and in Christ everything he does is pleasing to God (Apology IV, 140, 166, 172, 177, 308, 359, 375). These are the blessings which always accompany God's verdict of justification.

What the Lutherans viewed as necessary concomitants and fruits of justification Rome insisted were an essential part of the process itself. Trent states (Ses. VI, chap. 7) that justification "is the remission of sins but also the sanctification and renewal of the inner man through the voluntary reception of the grace and gifts whereby the unrighteous man becomes righteous and from being an enemy becomes a friend." Like the Lutheran position, the Roman doctrine views justification as a change of status, but that change is not brought about by God's verdict and declaration of righteousness but gradually through the process of renewal. Thus, the Roman view subsumes the article of justification under the articles of sanctification, renewal, and grace, and does so by divesting it of its meaning and identifying it with its effects so that cause and effect coalesce in the process.[67] In effect, by contending that justification is more than God's forensic act in declaring the sinner righteous for Christ's sake, Rome asserts that justification is not a forensic act at all.

Rome objected strenuously to the Lutheran doctrine that justification was the forgiveness of sins and the imputation of Christ's righteousness to the believer since this doctrine made justification unreal, no more than a putative judgment, and therefore a fiction. This argument was based on the assumption that a man's righteousness *must* be based on his own inherent righteousness and works of righteousness; otherwise any intrinsic declaration of God is not possible. Luther's doctrine of imputed righteousness was severely criticized as "insane and demented," a "spectrum of his brain," a "masked righteousness," an "encrusted righteousness, similar to the incrustation on whited sepulchers."[68] Steeped in rhetoric, the criticism asserted that the Lutheran doctrine made God's imputation an empty verdict, unreal, and merely putative.

Luther had answered his critics emphatically already in his day. He appealed to the almighty power and mercy of God who declares the sinner righteous. In his "Disputation on Justification" in 1536[69] he says,

> [Our adversaries] simply don't believe in the incredible greatness of God's power and in His mercy heaped upon mercy, mercy which would discount the one who is righteous, but count as righteous the one who is not righteous. This imputation is not a thing of no consequence, but is greater than the whole world, yea, than all the holy angels. Reason cannot see this, for reason disregards the Word of God; but we (I say) give thanks to God that we have such a Savior who is able to pass us by and reckon our sin as nothing.

Luther's words accomplished very little to satisfy his critics, and the polemics intensified after the Formula of Concord appeared. For the next two centuries Lutheran dogmaticians and exegetes were compelled to address the misunderstandings about this imputation again and again in order to clarify and defend their position. Friedrich Balduin, professor of exegesis at Wittenberg in the late seventeenth century, approaches the issue from an exegetical point of view, analyzing what an imputation is.[70] He points out that an imputation in the nature of the case is not a mere opinion. Neither can it be construed as a grafting or indwelling of one reality into another. Rather it is a cognitive act (*imputatio cognitionis*), a determinative act (*imputatio decreti*), whereby a "foreign *reality* is *really* applied and attributed to someone."

> This term imputation is borrowed from logic where a calculation has its validity not in itself but in its context. And so a cognitive or determinative imputation has two sides to it. First, it becomes the imputation of a thing by one person to another, in this case the righteousness of Christ to us and our unrighteousness in turn to Him, and this transfer takes place solely by the determination and judgment of God. According to this understanding, Paul writes that the righteousness of Christ is imputed to us and our sins to Christ (2 Corinthians 5:21). In this imputation something absent is received and possessed instead of something present, for the righteousness of Christ which is not in us is reckoned by God to be in us and our sin which is not in Christ is reckoned by God to be in Him. Second, it is an imputation of value and worth whereby the value and worth of one's things are transferred to another by a reckoning or determination, and this in such a way that he has the place and status of the other; just as the intercession of a criminal begs for the status of innocence, the faith of the believer seeks the status of righteousness. In this sense faith is said to be imputed for righteousness as though the person himself were righteous in himself because he has received upon request the righteousness of another.

John Andrew Quenstedt, the most celebrated Lutheran dogmatician of the seventeenth century, addressed the concept of the imputation more thoroughly than any other Lutheran theologian after the Formula of Concord, and he defended at great length the reality of the imputation and the reality of Christ's righteousness which was imputed to the believer.[71] He addressed the question, "whether in justification the righteousness of Christ is imputed to us":

> The righteousness of Christ is not our own formal righteousness. Neither is it a righteousness that inheres in us subjectively but is our real and sufficient righteousness by imputation. We do not through this

righteousness become righteous by a righteousness inhering in us, but through the imputation of this righteousness we are formally justified in such a way that without it there is no substance of our righteousness before God. From this fact that the righteousness of God is extrinsic to us we conclude that it does not dwell in us formally and intrinsically. And yet it does not follow therefore that righteousness cannot be reckoned to us extrinsically and objectively. For certainly our sins were extrinsic to Christ, and yet they could be imputed for punishment and guilt to Him and reckoned to Him.[72]

Quenstedt, taking a different approach from that of Balduin, answers the Roman Catholic objection to the doctrine of imputed righteousness by elaborating on what is meant by imputation and what is not meant.

We must distinguish between a mere putative righteousness which denies the reality of the righteousness and imputed righteousness which can be reckoned to others. The righteousness of Christ which has been reckoned to us is in itself neither putative nor fictitious, but absolutely real corresponding exactly to God's mind and will expressed in the Law, nor as a reckoning is it a mere act of imputing something, but is an absolutely real judgment of God which is rendered from the throne of grace through the Gospel in respect to the sinner who believes in Christ.[73]

When does the imputation of Christ's righteousness take place? It did not take place when Christ, by doing and suffering, finished His work of atonement and reconciled the world to God. Then and there, when the sins of the world were imputed to Him and He took them, Christ became our righteousness and procured for us remission of sins, justification, and eternal life. "By thus making satisfaction He procured and merited (*acquisivit et promeruit*) for each and every man remission of all sins, exemption from all punishments of sin, grace and peace with God, eternal righteousness and salvation."[74] But the imputation of Christ's righteousness to the sinner takes place when the Holy Spirit brings him to faith through Baptism and the Word of the Gospel. Our sins were imputed to Christ at His suffering and death, imputed objectively after He, by His active and passive obedience, fulfilled and *procured* all righteousness for us. But the imputation of His righteousness to us takes place when we are brought to faith.[75] Quenstedt says:

It is not just the same thing to say, "Christ's righteousness is imputed to us" and to say "Christ is our righteousness." For the imputation did not take place when Christ became our righteousness. The righteousness of Christ is the effect of His office. The imputation is the application of the effect of His office. The one, however, does not do away with the other. Christ is our righteousness effectively when He justifies us. His righteousness is ours objectively because our faith rests in Him. His righteousness is ours formally in that His righteousness is imputed to us.[76]

Quenstedt's great concern in presenting the doctrine of imputed righteousness against the Roman Catholic objection is to establish that both the righteousness of Christ and the imputation of His righteousness are real. We cite one final statement in which he explains his position.

This imputation is most real (*realissima*), whether viewed from the standpoint of the righteousness which is imputed or the act of imputing. The righteousness of Christ consisting in His doing and suffering is absolutely true and real (*verissima et realissima*). And this is what is imputed to us and corresponds precisely to God's mind and will which is expressed in the Law. The act of imputing, or the imputation itself, is also real because its measure is the infallible mind of God. Thus, God cannot regard or consider him to be just to whom true righteousness has not been appropriated; nor can there proceed from God's will, which is the norm of all goodness, any approval of a fictitious reckoning or righteousness. And so those to whom the righteousness of Christ is imputed are truly righteous, although not inherently or by inherence, but imputatively and through an extrinsic designation that they are such, for also from that which is extrinsic a true designation can take place. Therefore it is a vain question, whether we are really righteous by that imputation or whether we are only regarded as righteous. For God's judgment is according to truth. Therefore he who is regarded by God as righteous is truly righteous.[77]

The reality of the imputation of Christ's righteousness is at the very heart of the Lutheran doctrine of justification. Therefore Quenstedt makes so much of the fact. It is precisely at this point that the Gospel of the Second Article, the redemptive work of Christ, enters the doctrine of justification. And it is this connection of the work of

Christ to the justification of the sinner before God that makes the article of justification by faith the *praecipuus locus* of the evangelical doctrine, yes, makes it the Gospel of justification.

At bottom, there are three possible interpretations of what takes place when the sinner is accounted (imputed) righteous. All three interpretations, or views, of the imputation were already clearly present at the time of the Reformation. *First* was the position of some of the medieval nominalists, and more prominently of the Socinians, who taught an "absolute grace," a free and absolute imputation which did not require the intervention of Christ to atone for the sins of the world. Quenstedt comments, "Scripture never teaches that God forgives sin by absolute grace."[78] The "pious" *gratia absoluta* of the Socinians was a denial of Christ and the Gospel, and, ironically, of grace itself.[79] *Second* was the position of Trent and Rome that in the imputation of righteousness God reckons a person to be righteous because he is righteous, or, more accurately, because he is becoming righteous. God imputes to man what He already is. The imputation as such *effects* nothing. It is a simple *analytic* judgment, such as any human judge might render. *Third* was the Lutheran position. The imputation is a *synthetic* judgment which, because it is God's almighty and gracious reckoning and verdict, is effective and creative. The imputation makes a sinner righteous. Melanchthon means just this when he says that the verdict of justification "makes" (*effici*) righteous men out of unrighteous men (Apology IV, 72).[80]

There is a world of difference between the three interpretations concerning what the imputation of righteousness is. The Socinians and nominalists leave Christ out of the picture totally. The Roman Catholic view relegates Christ's atoning work to the background of what takes place as a sinner is declared righteous. But all three sides have a basis for the imputation of righteousness to the sinner. For the Socinians it is God's absolute grace. For the Roman Catholics it is the incipient righteousness (*justitia inchoata*) of the believer. For the Lutherans the basis of the imputation, as well as what is actually imputed to the believer, is the foreign righteousness of Christ. In all fairness to the position of all three parties, they taught clearly that the basis of God's justification and His reckoning the sinner to be righteous, the basis of the imputation and the imputation itself, were real.

Quenstedt's incisive explanation and argument for the reality of the imputed righteousness and the many other thorough discussions of the subject by Lutheran and Reformed theologians went unheeded by Roman Catholic theologians and officials. For the next three centuries the Roman Catholic Church continued to repeat the same arguments against the Lutheran position and perpetuate the same caricatures of it. In the mid-nineteenth century Cardinal Perrone, perhaps the most celebrated Jesuit of the day, was still repeating the same caricature, probably based on the writings of Cardinal Bellarmine and other sixteenth century Jesuit fathers. He said, "According to the doctrine of the Protestants it does not happen that sins are remitted at all, but are merely concealed according to an extrinsic imputation of the righteousness of God or Christ. And thus by the power of justification there begins to take place in us a certain inner renewal by which men become inwardly and formally righteous from sin."[81] This brief statement represents a complete misrepresentation of the Lutheran position at every point. No amount of patient explanation of the Protestant position made any dent on Roman Catholic theologians until very recently.[82]

Why did Roman Catholic theologians so vehemently and consistently represent the Lutheran doctrine of imputed righteousness as a fiction? Why did the Lutherans just as vehemently and consistently insist that the imputation of Christ's righteousness to the believer was "absolutely real," as Quenstedt said? Not only polemical motives were involved. And certainly the Lutherans did not reaffirm their position so emphatically merely out of party spirit or because they saw validity in the Roman Catholic arguments. They considered the arguments obstinate and absurd. Rather, the Lutherans saw the Roman polemic at just this point, even though it was weak, to be attacking the very heart of the evangelical doctrine of justification. And Rome agreed. Rome saw clearly that the doctrine of imputed righteousness struck at the very heart of the Roman doctrine of grace and sanctification.

It is very disappointing to observe how little attention the Lutheran participants in the dialogues on justification have given the doctrine of imputed righteousness, to say nothing of the reality of the imputation.

It is especially disappointing in the light of the strong emphasis in the various statements on the importance and reality of renewal, at times regarded as a part of justification.

The Lutheran is troubled that *On Justification* so often calls justification "one image among the many used to set forth the significance of God's deed in Jesus Christ" (4), one picture among the many used in Scripture to serve as an "interpretation of the Christ event," a picture which need not be used in presenting the Gospel and can be replaced in our day. Thus, the reality of a divine imputation of Christ's righteousness to the believer is left in doubt and in fact is never discussed in *On Justification* at all.

A confessional Lutheran is heartened by an excellent statement in *Justification by Faith* (par. 98) on forensic justification and the imputed *justitia aliena*. The statement is worth citing:

> Lutherans describe justification as the imputation to sinners of the righteousness which is that of Christ Himself (*justitia aliena*), received in faith. Justification is the forensic act whereby God declares the sinner just; it is an act performed outside of us (*extra nos*) by which faith is accounted as righteousness. Looking on God's declaration as efficacious, Lutherans also affirm the reality of sanctification and good works, but they regard these effects as fruits rather than parts of justification itself. In this sense the Lutheran doctrine of imputed righteousness is intended to safeguard the unconditional character of God's promises in Christ.

We must bear in mind, however, that the statement expresses only the historic Lutheran teaching and does not state that the righteousness imputed to the believer is the obedience of Christ's doing and suffering. The statement is followed by a statement of the Roman Catholic doctrine which concludes with the words (*Justification by Faith*, par. 99), "But Catholics hesitate to trace everything to justification which is considered simply as a forensic act. They are often inclined to emphasize other images and concepts such as the remission of sins, adoption, redemption, regeneration, healing, sanctification, reconciliation, new creation, and salvation." The two statements are placed side by side, and no attempt is made to reconcile them.

The Lutheran might at first also be heartened when he reads that in the final presentation of "Material Convergences" between Lutherans and Roman Catholics (*Justification by Faith,* Par. 156) it is affirmed that justification "is not a legal fiction." But nowhere in the "Convergences" does *Justification by Faith* define justification as a forensic act. And when in the same context *Justification by Faith* states that "God, in justifying, effects what He promises; He forgives sin and makes us truly righteous" (which expresses the Tridentine understanding of justification), then it is renewal which is said to be not fictitious, rather than the imputation of Christ's righteousness. So a Lutheran is again troubled with the lack of any forthright *confession* of the Reformation doctrine in *Justification by Faith.*[83]

Finally, a Lutheran is troubled by the fact that *Joint Declaration,* which purports to be a consensus document, says nothing about the imputation of Christ's righteousness in justification at all. It merely states that God declares and makes believers righteous and does not impute sins to them, an assertion which in its context is more compatible with Trent than with the Lutheran Confessions,[84] hardly enough for a consensus document.

# Ten

# Faith, Justifying Faith, Faith Alone

The last term which completes the brief formulation of the Lutheran doctrine of justification which has been considered throughout this study is the term "faith." In the case of this term, too, Rome and the Lutherans were in utter disagreement and attached entirely different meanings to the word. A deep controversy arose at the time of the Reformation concerning what faith is and what it has to do with the justification of a sinner before God. In the light of this controversy two questions are pertinent: 1) What is faith when considered in the context of justification? 2) What is the function or role of faith in the justification of a sinner? These two questions entail each other and are inextricably conjoined and interrelated. To answer the one is to answer the other.

1. The term justifying faith (*fides justificans*), used by Melanchthon in the Apology occasionally and once in the Formula of Concord (Epitome III, 11), gained coinage in the late sixteenth and seventeenth centuries. Trent (VI, 6) also used the expression without prejudice in response to the Lutheran teaching concerning what faith was in reference to justification. What, then, is justifying faith in Lutheran theology? Or to put the question according to the German text of Melanchthon's Apology of the Augsburg Confession (Apology IV, 61): What Is the Faith Which Makes Us Holy and Righteous before God?

When the Lutheran Confessions refer to "the faith that justifies," they are speaking discretely and ruling out many aspects of faith and usages of the word commonly found in Scripture and/or theological discourse. They are not speaking or thinking of faith as it relates to prayer (Augsburg Confession X, 37), or hope (Apology IV, 48, 346), or to the fruits of the Spirit (Augsburg Confession IV, 1; Apology IV, 392; Formula of Concord. Epitome VI, 6), or of faith as it bears the cross (Augsburg Confession XX, 37), or of faith as a knowledge of theological matters (Augsburg Confession XX, 26; Apology IV, 383).

They are not referring to "general faith" (*fides generalis*) which holds to all the articles of the Christian doctrine (Apology XII, 45), a faith that believes that God exists (Apology XII, 60) and believes the historical events pertaining to Christ's death (Augsburg Confession XX, 22; Apology IV, 17), often called a "historical knowledge" (Apology IV, 48, 50, 61; cf. Apology IV, 337, 383). No, when the Lutheran Confessions speak of justifying faith they are referring to *trust* (*fiducia*), trust in the promise of God's mercy which saves us (Apology IV, 330) for Christ's sake (Apology IV, 79, 118, 383; Formula of Concord, Solid Declaration IV, 12). Such trust is directed toward God Himself; it is trust in God Himself; it is trust in Christ's merits (Apology IV, 16); it "lays hold on the name of Christ" (Apology IV, 98), a trust which actually apprehends the mercy of God offered in the Word (Apology IV, 157).

Another word often used in the Lutheran Confessions to describe justifying faith is the word "*confidence*," confidence in God's grace alone (Apology IV, 381) and in the Gospel (Large Catechism III, 89). Still another synonym of justifying faith, sometimes portrayed as the result of faith and trust (Apology IV, 205), sometimes as faith itself (Augsburg Confession XX, 26), is the term "assurance" (*consolatio*), assurance of God's grace and salvation (Large Catechism III, 95; Formula of Concord, Epitome XI, 13; Solid Declaration IV, 37). Such assurance is given through Word and Sacrament (Solid Declaration VII, 62, 116; XI, 72).

Often justifying faith is called knowledge in the Lutheran Confessions. "This faith is the true knowledge of Christ," Melanchthon says (Apology IV, 46). But to know Christ is not "merely" (Apology IV, 48) to have an idle, historic knowledge about Him (Apology IV, 61, 99, 337), but to have a Spirit-wrought knowledge that Christ is Savior. "What is the knowledge of Christ, except to know Christ's blessings, the promises which by the Gospel He has spread throughout the world? And to know these blessings is rightly and truly to believe in Christ, to believe that God will certainly accomplish what He has promised for Christ's sake" (Apology IV, 101).

This understanding of faith as not merely *notitia*, a knowledge of events and facts concerning Jesus, but a *cognitio*, a personal knowledge of Christ Himself, introduces the notion of what Luther and

Melanchthon call personal faith or special faith (*fides specialis*). Melanchthon says (Apology IV, 45), "Therefore, when a man believes that his sins are forgiven to him because of Christ, . . . this personal faith obtains the forgiveness of sins and justifies us." Melanchthon then adds a significant sentence: "In penitence and the terrors of conscience it consoles and encourages our hearts." Here Melanchthon sets personal faith, justifying faith, squarely within the context of repentance and the preaching of Law and Gospel and the work of the Holy Spirit, working contrition and sorrow for sins through the Law and faith and trust in Christ through the Gospel. The nature of justifying faith can only be understood in the light of repentance.

In speaking of justifying faith the Lutheran Confessions are summarizing what Melanchthon had already discussed at greater length in his various editions of the *Loci Communes* and Chemnitz in greater detail in his *Loci Theologici* and his *Examination of the Council of Trent.*[85] Melanchthon in his *Loci Communes* goes to great pains to prove from Scripture that the word "faith" must always be understood as "trusting that we have been received by mercy for the sake of Christ, and not because of our own virtues." When used in the context of justification, the New Testament word *pisteuō* always means "to trust" in agreement with the classical usage of the word, which has the force of assenting to something and trusting in something.

Chemnitz[86] follows the same line of argument but in far greater detail. He asserts on the basis of numerous examples from the Old and New Testaments that faith in someone (God) or something (God's promises) means trust. Even when the object of faith is something external and only tangentially related to forgiveness and salvation (e.g., answer to prayer), the element of trust is always dominant. The many attributes ascribed to faith indicate that justifying faith is essentially trust. Chemnitz points out how faith is called "an evidence (*hypostasis*) of things hoped for," that is, "a sure expectation." It is metaphorically called a "shield" (Ephesians 6:16), a "breastplate" (1 Thessalonians 5:8), a "fight" (1 Timothy 6:2), an "anchor" (Hebrews 6:19), and a "work" (1 Thessalonians 1:3). It is called "full assurance" (Romans 4:21; Hebrews 6:17), a "persuasion," "boldness," "confidence," and "certainty," which is the very antithesis of doubt.

Faith keeps "the Word of Christ" (John 8:51, 14:23), "guards" the Word (Luke 11:28), and "receives" the Word (Luke 18:13; 1 Timothy 1:4); it never judges, criticizes, or doubts it (Romans 4:20; Acts 10:20; Matthew 8:26). No one ever probed into the biblical meaning of the concept of "faith" more deeply than did Martin Chemnitz.

When Lutheran theology defines faith essentially as trust, it always means trust in the Word of the Gospel, trust based on the cognitive Word and doctrine of the Gospel. This trust involves the whole man with all his faculties, his intellect and will as well as his heart.

Chemnitz points out[87] that when the Holy Spirit brings a person to faith through the Word and Sacrament so that the person lays hold on the promise and "takes possession" of it, there are four "movements" or "steps" (*gradus*), as it were, in what takes place. First, there is a knowledge, a thinking and meditation on the promise of God concerning the "blessings" (*beneficia*) of Christ pertaining to our salvation. Justifying faith is not mere historical knowledge or general faith. When Lutherans say that faith is knowing Christ's benefits, that is, that its "principal object" is the promise of grace, it does not "exclude the other parts of the heavenly doctrine,"[88] but "assents to the entire Word of God." However, "faith justifies only with respect to its object which is Christ." And the believer "refers all the other articles of the faith to the promise of grace for the sake of Christ the Mediator." The second movement of faith is assent. The believer concludes with firm persuasion that the universal promise of the Gospel is meant for him and that he is included in it (Romans 4:23-24). The third movement of justifying faith is the movement of the heart and will of the believer which wants and seeks forgiveness of sins and the blessings of justification held forth in the Gospel. And from the third follows the fourth movement which is confidence in the grace of God offered in the Gospel. All four of these "movements" (*motus*) of justifying faith are aspects of trust in Christ, aspects of personal faith.

For the next two centuries all the Lutheran teachers placed great emphasis on the confessional understanding of saving faith as trust. And they often expressed eloquently the comfort derived from this understanding of faith as trust, set in the context of Law and Gospel. Thus, Jesper Brochmand says:[89]

> Justifying faith is true knowledge and firm assent to the divine Word. It is first and foremost the heart's unhesitating confidence that in all

necessities, even when the entire soul is quaking because of sin, the poor sinner can conclude with all certainty that God wishes to forgive sins for the sake of His Son Jesus, not just the sins of others, but his own sins, even though he is the greatest of sinners, and that God reckons to him Christ's righteousness and gives him eternal life.

A generation later Abraham Calov writes in the same vein:[90]

Justifying faith is our confidence in divine mercy in Christ, it is trust in Jesus, assurance that He has paid for our sins, restored us to righteousness and gained eternal life for us; and it is therefore confidence that for Christ's sake God forgives us our sins and in His grace wishes to rescue us for an inheritance of eternal life.

The later Lutheran teachers, however, reduced Chemnitz's four "movements" of justifying faith to three: knowledge (*notitia*), assent, and trust. David Hollaz, the last of the great confessional Lutheran dogmaticians, who wrote during the age of pietism and was affected by it, presented the later Lutheran understanding on the movements of justifying faith. His position (which seems quite fair to Chemnitz's treatment but does not improve upon it) has become standard to this day among confessional Lutherans. He says:[91] "The activities, steps, and parts of justifying faith, through which faith apprehends its object, are three: knowledge, assent, and trust." Hollaz cites the Lutheran Confessions and Chemnitz and observes that the three elements of justifying faith are all found in 1 Timothy 1:15-16. Knowledge is indicated in the words, "Christ Jesus came into this world to save sinners"; assent in the words, "this is a faithful saying and worthy of all acceptation"; and trust in the words, "I am the chief," and "in me first." Hollaz is viewing justifying faith not merely in its beginning at the time of the sinner's conversion or regeneration, but in the ongoing life of a Christian who continues to trust in the mercy of Christ.[92]

Like the Confessions, all the later Lutheran teachers emphasized that trust is the very essence of justifying faith and must be present if there is to be faith at all. Knowledge and assent can obtain among heretics and unbelievers. Trust, a personal appropriation of the benefits of Christ, is the decisive factor.[93]

Trent (VI, canon 12) rejected the Lutheran teaching that justifying faith was trust in the grace and mercy of God for Christ's sake. "If anyone says that justifying faith is nothing else than trust in divine mercy, or that it is this trust alone by which we are justified, let him be anathema." Trent understood perfectly what the Lutheran position was on this point. Trent does not hesitate to speak of justifying faith and (using Pauline language) of justification by faith. But in opposition to the Lutheran doctrine, the Tridentine fathers described justifying faith according to the old scholastic pattern of thought as an infused virtue and a faith formed by love. Chapter 7 states, "For faith, unless hope, and love are joined (*accedat*) to it, neither unites perfectly with Christ nor makes one a living member of His body." Just previously the chapter had stated that man who is grafted into Christ receives in justification the remission of sins and at the same time "all these infused [virtues]: faith, hope, and love."

Nowhere do Trent or later Roman Catholic theologians define justifying faith as trust, at least not trust in the mercy of God. Rather, faith is considered a virtue which, along with hope and love, constitutes the beginning of the justification process (*Catholic Catechism*, 1814). Trust, however, was considered an element of faith. Even prior to Baptism, which is the instrumental cause of justification and without which no one has ever been justified (Trent, VI, chap. 7) or saved, one who is not yet engrafted into Christ can possess these virtues incipiently. Trust, then, or certitude, is akin to dogmatic faith, a firm conviction and acceptance of the dogmas of the faith and the authority of God who reveals them.[94] Considered relative to justification, it is not appropriate to be classified as receptivity. In the nature of the case, a virtue is a good work and does not function as a "receiving organ" of God's grace and mercy by which one is justified. It is in this sense that Trent understands the *per fidem* of Romans 3:28. Clearly, how one defines justifying faith and trust will determine how one understands the role faith plays in one's justification before God.

# Eleven

## The Object of Justifying Faith

What is the object of justifying faith in Lutheran theology? On what or whom does the Christian's faith depend? The answer to this question has already been given in discussion of the previous question, "What is justifying faith?"

Throughout the Four Gospels our Lord Jesus Christ presents Himself as the object of faith and promises forgiveness, life, and salvation to everyone who believes in Him. The same way of salvation was taught by the prophets in the Old Testament and the apostles in the New Testament.

> The patriarchs knew the promise of Christ, that for His sake God intended to forgive sins. As they understood that Christ would be the price for our sins, they knew that our works could not pay so high a price. Therefore they received free mercy and the forgiveness of sins by faith, just as the saints in the New Testament. (Apology IV, 57; XII, 53)

Syntactically, the objects of the verb *pisteuō* and other verbs for "believe" are quite diverse. Scripture speaks of believing in "the promises" (Galatians 3:16), the "Word" (Matthew 8:8; Titus 1:9), the "report" (Isaiah 53:1; Romans 10:16), the "Gospel" (Philippians 1:17), the "record" (1 John 5:10), etc. In every case, however, the object of saving faith is the content of the Word and promise and Gospel, namely, Christ the Mediator.

Our Lutheran Confessions speak in the same synecdochical fashion as do the Scriptures. Rather seldom is Christ the object of the verb "believe." More often faith is directed to the Word, the Gospel, the promises, or to Scripture (Large Catechism III, 31) as they preach Christ and point to Him and His work and His bringing forgiveness to believers (Augsburg Confession XIII, 2; Apology VII, 28). But more often still, the Lutheran Confessions portray justifying faith as believing *that* Christ suffered for us (Augsburg Confession IV, 2), *that* God is merciful and gracious and justifies the sinner and forgives and saves him for Christ's sake (Augsburg Confession XII, 5; Apology IV, 76, 179, 230, 267, 292, 382; XI, 2), or *that* we are received into fellowship with God when we believe in Christ (Augsburg Confession IV, 2; V, 3; XXVII, 37). In the theology of Luther and the Lutheran Confessions, as in Scripture, to believe with saving faith in God or in Christ (cf. Small Catechism and Large Catechism II) is to believe all kinds of things about our gracious God and what He has done to save us. If you do not believe that God is gracious and that He sent His Son to save you and that He gives you His Holy Spirit to sanctify you, you have no faith at all.

The upshot of the Lutheran doctrine, drawn from the Scriptures, is that saving faith in God is faith in His Son who lived and died to save sinners. And this is the same as believing in the Gospel which tells you what God has done for Christ's sake; it is the same as believing in the forgiveness of sins, life in Christ, and salvation. Quenstedt puts it well:[95]

> When the terms grace or mercy of God are set forth as the object of our trust, this does not exclude Christ our Mediator and His atonement for our sins from being the object of our faith, but includes it. Contrariwise, when Christ our Mediator is designated as the object of faith, this does not exclude the grace of God . . . but includes it and lets it be tacitly understood.

David Hollaz says much the same thing:[96]

> The object of faith is in reality always the same, whether we describe it as Christ the Mediator, or as the grace of God, or as the gracious promise made for the sake of Christ the Mediator. The difference is merely one of conception and expression.

Furthermore, there is no difference between believing God when He speaks promises and believing *in God*. "Abraham believed God (Genesis 15:6) in such a way that Abraham believed in God, believed in Him as the One who promises things gratuitously and gives the righteousness by which the things promised are bestowed."[97]

Personal saving faith is directed toward the mercy of God and toward Christ the Mediator and in no way negates or depreciates the importance of pure doctrine in directing faith to its object. After all, it is the Gospel, the teaching of the Gospel (*doctrinae evangelii*), along with the Sacraments, which are the only means to bring a poor sinner to faith in Christ and the mercy of God. And there is a definite doctrinal content to the propositions of the Gospel and to the proposition that faith is directed to Christ the Redeemer and to the grace and mercy of God.[98]

Quenstedt responds to Cardinal Bellarmine who identified the object of faith as the Word of God in the wide sense or the entire revelation of God, and to the Socinians, who, as Unitarians, taught that the object of saving faith was God and only in a secondary sense considered Christ the object of faith. He says:[99]

> The proper and adequate object of justifying faith, insofar as faith is trust, and the source where faith seeks and receives the remission of sins and life eternal, is God's special (*specialis*) grace brought to us in Christ, or, to say the same thing, the Gospel promise concerning the grace of God in Christ.

It is noteworthy that both conservative Rome and the liberal Socinians—both ends of the theological spectrum—denied a) that faith was trust, and b) that the object of faith was God who is gracious toward us for Christ's sake. As far as can be discerned, Rome has not deviated from its position to this day. And the Socinian teaching that faith was a firm "opinion" rather than a firm "trust," together with the denial of the vicarious atonement of Christ, finds broad representation throughout modern liberal Protestantism. Lutheranism tries to wend a middle path between the dogmatic faith of Roman Catholics attributed to Trent and Bellarmine and the generic faith of the Socinians devoid of all evangelical content.

In his *Fundamentals of Catholic Doctrine* (p. 251), Ludwig Ott speaks for the Roman Catholic Church today on this important matter.

> As far as the content of justifying faith is concerned, the so-called fiducial faith does not suffice, but rather, what is demanded is theological or dogmatic faith (confessional faith) which consists in the firm

acceptance of the divine truths of revelation, on the authority of God revealing. The Council of Trent declares: *Si quis dixerit, fidem iustificantem nihil aliud esse quam fiduciam divinae misericordiae . . .* A.S. D 822.

It is worth noting that Ott cites the following passages in proof of his contention that justifying faith is dogmatic faith: Mark 16:16; John 20:31; Hebrews 11:6; John 3:14 ff. It should be pointed out that every one of these citations points to Christ according to His person and work as the object of faith. Ott does not deny that faith has in it an element of trust, but, like Trent, he categorically makes the object of justifying faith the dogmas of the church or the entire revelation. Justifying faith is directed toward doctrine. Faith is, at bottom, *fides generalis*. It appears that the Roman Catholic representatives in all the recent dialogues with Lutherans have not departed from this position, although they have couched their opinion in terminology more congenial to Lutherans at many points.

On the other side of the spectrum today lies liberal Protestantism, existential theology, pietism (often among Lutherans), and other subjective theologies which, for one reason or another, stress the personal nature of faith to the point that God or Christ is the object of faith almost entirely to the exclusion of anything that can be said about Christ and His work. Either from a distrust of the very concept of pure doctrine based upon Scripture or from a distaste toward orthodoxy and confessionalism of any kind, theologians retreat into a personalistic, quasi-mystical view of faith, often coupled with a denial of revealed theology (Emil Brunner, John Baillie, et al.). Such a view can only become introspective and subjectivistic, preoccupied more with faith and the "dynamics of faith" (Tillich) than the object of faith. Such a theology—if it can be called a theology at all and not merely anthropology—we see not only in liberal Protestantism, Neo-Orthodoxy, and Bultmannian Existentialism but also in Protestant Fundamentalism, Pentecostalism, Pop-Evangelicalism, Revivalism, and the modern Church Growth Movement (which has made deep inroads into every segment of Christianity including the Roman Catholic Church). This personalistic view of faith tends to be fideistic and synergistic. Faith is turned into an emotion, an experience, a "decision," something self-contrived, an effort of man, without substance (Hebrew 11:1) or foundation in any sure and certain object. Perhaps Karl Barth's judgment of much of modern theology is not too harsh: "A self-fabricated faith is the climax of unbelief."[100]

Francis Pieper[101] speaks out against the more conservative positive theologians of his day on this matter. These theologians made the atonement of Christ immaterial as a factor in leading faith to its object. He says:

> It is the fundamental error of modern positive theologians when they make the person of Christ the object of faith to the exclusion of the work of Christ, i.e., His fulfillment of the Law and His suffering of the penalty of the Law in the place of man. This error does away with the biblical object of faith, indeed with faith itself. We do not believe in Christ to our justification and salvation unless we believe in Him as the One who was crucified for the expiation of our sins (1 Corinthians 2:2), shed His precious blood (1 Peter 1:18), gave His life into death (Matthew 10:28; Romans 5:10), and in our stead fulfilled the Law (Galatians 4:4-5).

Confessional Lutheranism sees the remedy for this deplorable situation, whether found in Romanism or various schools of Protestantism, in restoring Christ and His saving work (the *solus Christus*) as the center and total content of saving faith. Faith has its existence in its object. Railing against the notion that faith is a virtue formed by love whose object is doctrine and not Christ and His righteousness, Luther expresses his Christocentric doctrine of justification at this point. For years Luther went despairing because he sought certainty of salvation in his own feeling and contrition and faith. It was only after he abandoned the *fides formata* and discovered that faith saves because it grasps the precious pearl Jesus Christ that Luther found peace. He says:[102]

> Therefore what the sophists say about justifying faith being furnished with love is nothing but an idle fiction. For it is the faith which grasps Christ the Son of God and is furnished with Him which justifies, not the faith which includes love. Faith if it is to be sure and firm must grasp nothing else than Christ alone. In distress and terrors of conscience faith has nothing other to lean on than this. So the one who takes Christ by

faith, even if he is terrified by the Law and sorely oppressed by sins, can still boast that he is righteous. How can he do this, and through what means? Through the pearl Christ whom he has by faith.

Luther's emphasis on the *solus Christus* as the focus of the Christian's faith was reflected in the preaching, church life, and hymnody of the Lutheran Church until the time of the Enlightenment. After that time the better pietists and confessional Lutherans have kept this focus alive to this day. This Christocentric understanding of faith and its object and of the Christian religion can be seen most clearly in the great Lutheran chorales and hymns of the sixteenth and seventeenth centuries. These typified the doctrine and life of the Lutheran Church in those centuries. Two stanzas from J. H. Schroeder's hymn, "One Thing's Needful," written in the early years of the age of pietism—or the waning years of orthodoxy—illustrate this Christocentric theology that is found really only in the Lutheran hymnody.

> I have naught, my God, to offer,
> Save the blood of Thy dear Son;
> Graciously accept the proffer:
> Make His righteousness mine own.
> His holy life gave He, was crucified for me;
> His righteousness perfect He now pleads before Thee;
> His own robe of righteousness, my highest good,
> Shall clothe me in glory, through faith in His blood.
>
> Jesus, in Thy cross are centered
> All the marvels of Thy grace;
> Thou, my Savior, once hast entered
> Through Thy blood the holy place:
> Thy sacrifice holy there wrought my redemption,
> From Satan's dominion I now have exemption;
> The way is now free to the Father's high throne,
> Where I may approach Him in Thy name alone.

Verses from Schroeder's magnificent hymn, centering in Christ's righteousness as the content of the Christian's faith, are typical of almost two hundred years of Lutheran hymnody. These great hymns were not merely prayers. They were not merely doxology. They were confessions of faith, the faith of Christ's church in Christ's Gospel, and even more, they expressed the personal faith (*fides specialis*) of millions of Christians who sang them. It is sad to note that these great Lutheran hymns are not sung much anymore in Lutheran churches. Perhaps they are considered too drab (many are written in a minor key), too long (Schroeder's hymn is ten stanzas, and some of the hymns were still longer), too difficult to sing, or too doctrinal. Perhaps this present situation is just one example of how Lutherans today have lost their Christocentric focus as well as their theological interest.

# Twelve

# Faith's Part in Justification

Our justification before God is received and apprehended through faith. All through Scripture faith is represented as the receiving organ (*organon lēptikon*) for all the blessings of God. And the greatest of all God's benefits is His righteousness, which is received "by faith (*dia pisteōs*) of Jesus Christ unto all and upon all them that believe" (Romans 3:22). Again in Romans 3:25 we are told that these great benefits are received through faith in His blood (*dia pisteōs en tō autou haimati*). The object of faith in this case is the blood, which is to be understood synecdochically for the entire obedience and suffering of Christ. The *dia* points to the same means through which the results of this atoning and propitiatory blood become ours. Scripture expresses in many ways how faith is the one means by which we *receive* Christ's righteousness, forgiveness, and the grace of God, the one means through which we are justified (*pistei*: Romans 3:28; Acts 26:18; *ek pisteōs*: Romans 3:30, 5:1; Galatians 2:16, 3:7-9, 11-12; *dia tēs pisteōs*: Romans 3:31).[103]

It is notable how often Scripture speaks of faith as a receiving, an accepting, a taking, an apprehending; but it is always the receiving and apprehending of *something*. In John 1:12, Romans 5:17, and Galatians 3 the believer receives (*lambanein*) Christ, "the abundance of grace," and "the promise of the Spirit." In John 1:5 the believer receives (*katalambanein*) "the light." In John 1:11 the believer receives (*paralambanein*) Christ. In Luke 8:13 and Acts 8:14 the believer receives (*dechesthai*) "the word." In Acts 2:41 the believer receives (*apodechesthai*) "the word." In 1 Timothy 1:14 the believer receives (*apodechesthai*) "the faithful word."

On the basis of the biblical data just reviewed, the Lutheran Confessions conclude as follows. Since all the benefits of Christ (forgiveness, righteousness, salvation, etc.) are offered in the Word and promises of the Gospel and are offered to be received by faith, faith is the appropriate vehicle and means to receive such gifts and blessings.

How else does the sinner receive a verdict of acquittal except by faith?
The Formula of Concord (Solid Declaration III, 10-12) says:

> The Holy Spirit offers these treasures to us in the promise of the
> Gospel, and faith is the only means whereby we can apprehend, accept,
> apply them to ourselves, and make them our own. Faith is a gift of God
> whereby we rightly learn to know Christ as our Redeemer in the Word of
> the Gospel and to trust in Him, but solely for the sake of His obedience
> we have forgiveness of sins by grace, are accounted righteous and holy by
> God the Father, and are saved forever. Thus, the following statements of
> St. Paul are to be considered and taken as synonymous: "we are justified
> by faith" (Romans 3:28), or "faith is reckoned to us as righteousness"
> (Romans 4:5), or when he says that we are justified by the obedience of
> Christ, our only Mediator, or that "one man's righteousness leads to
> acquittal and life for all men" (Romans 5:18).

Faith receives the gifts of forgiveness and salvation and all the
gifts of God. We are reminded of Luther's statement cited above:
"Faith holds out the hand and the sack and just lets the good be done to
it. For as God is the Giver who bestows such things in His love, we are
the receivers who receive the gift through faith which does nothing."[104]
Lutheran theologians since the time of the Reformation have often
likened the activity—or rather passivity—of justifying faith to the
activity—or rather passivity—of an empty hand. Elling Hove[105] says,

> The believer becomes righteous in the same way as a beggar may be
> made rich by a gift. Through the acceptance of the gift it becomes his.
> The acceptance of the gift does not merit the gift . . . Whether he accepts
> it with a feeble or a strong, firm hand, the value of the gift is the same.

Quenstedt employs the same sort of analogy.[106]

> When the hand of a starving man seizes bread which is offered him, it
> is not this taking of the bread which satisfies the man, for he could seize a
> piece of mud or stone or something else which could not satisfy him; but
> his being satisfied depends on the object which he takes to himself and
> depends on his eating it, that is to say, it depends on the bread. When the
> lips of a thirsty man drink water which has been drawn with a vessel from
> some well, it is not the drinking as such that quenches his thirst, for you
> can also draw sand or blood with a vessel. No, if his thirst is to be

quenched, the drink which he consumes must have the power to quench thirst. Thus, he who hungers and thirsts after righteousness receives it through faith, as the begging hand which receives bread coming down from heaven (John 6:50-51) and the vessel of the living soul draws the water springing up into everlasting life (John 4:14); but it is not this receiving and drinking as such which drives away the spiritual hunger and quenches the thirst. Man does not possess anything of such a nature as can accomplish all this, e.g., his own merits, his own pretended autonomy, satisfactions which are the invention of the synagogue of Rome. No, the whole strength of man's receiving depends on the thing which is received through faith, the redemption, and the blood of Jesus Christ.

Quenstedt is saying that faith justifies not because it receives, but because of *what* it receives, because of its *object*. Faith does not justify in itself (*in se et in sua natura*) because it is my act, my stepping out and accepting something, but totally by virtue of the gift given me to receive. Faith insofar as it is our acceptance (*quatenus est apprehensio*) could be the apprehension of something imaginary or of our own human righteousness. Such faith would never justify. Quenstedt is reflecting a fundamental point and concern of Luther and the Lutheran Confessions. The Formula of Concord says (Solid Declaration III, 13),

> For faith does not justify because it is so good a work and so God-pleasing a virtue, but because it lays hold of and accepts the merit of Christ and the promise of the Holy Gospel. This merit has to be applied to us and to be made our own through faith if we are to be justified thereby. Therefore the righteousness which by grace is reckoned to faith or to the believer is the obedience, the passion, and the resurrection of Christ when He satisfied the Law for us and paid for our sins.[107]

Before the Formula of Concord was written, Jacob Heerbrand[108] had voiced the same practical concern.

> Faith is not a human persuasion, which some falsely ascribe to us, a persuasion which would in every case fail. No, it is a work of God and gift of the Holy Spirit in us. We are not justified by faith insofar as it is a quality in us, as again the enemies of God's grace, the Neo-Pelagians, falsely accuse us of teaching, namely, that the unrighteous are justified when they have a certain idea (or rather dream) that they are righteous. No, we are justified by faith insofar as it apprehends Christ who for us

was made righteousness by God, sanctification and redemption, and insofar as faith is concerned applies Christ's merit to itself.

One cannot fail to perceive how these many testimonies of Lutheran teachers of every era stress the importance of faith as the instrument, the empty hand which seizes the treasure that God offers. If this is not the case, Christians may be tempted to trust in their own faith (because they think it is strong or pleasing to God) rather than in the object of their faith, which is Christ. Or Christians may despair because they look within themselves for certainty and in their heart find only the weakest, faltering faith, whereas they should look to the promise and to Christ alone for certainty and hope of every good gift.[109]

# Thirteen

# Justification by Faith Alone

If faith is the only "means and instrument" through which we "receive and accept the grace of God, the merit of Christ, and the forgiveness of sins offered us in the promise of the Gospel" (Formula of Concord, Solid Declaration III, 31; cf. also Apology IV, 69), it is easy to understand why the doctrine of justification by faith alone was so important to the Lutherans. The *sola fide* was important for two very practical reasons. First, God wants us to be sure of the forgiveness of our sins (Romans 4:16). Second, God wants us to glory not in ourselves but in His grace (Ephesians 2:9).[110] The Formula of Concord eloquently expresses this deep soteriological concern.

> In order to afford saddened consciences dependable and reliable comfort and to give due honor to the merit of Christ and the grace of God, Scripture teaches that the righteousness of faith before God consists *solely* in the gracious reconciliation of the forgiveness of sins, which is bestowed upon us by *pure* grace because of the unique merit of Christ, the Mediator, and which we receive *only* by faith in the promise of the Gospel. (Solid Declaration III, 30)

We notice here that *sola gratia*, *solus Christus*, and *sola fide* are linked together and are dependent upon each other. It is only when this is the case that the comfort of the Gospel and the glory of Christ are maintained. Now what is the scriptural warrant for the *sola fide*?

The Lutheran Confessions and later Lutheran teachers respond to this question in great detail. *First*, they appeal to the biblical evidence that the cause within God which moves Him to justify sinners is always exclusively His grace and mercy. This fact excludes any human work or activity as the basis of justification and proves the *sola fide*. If justification is declared freely (*dōrean, gratis*) over the sinner by God's grace (Romans 3:24), then only faith is left to justify. Romans 11:6 states the principle: "And if by grace, then it is no more of works:

otherwise grace is no more grace. But if it be of works, then it is no more of grace: otherwise work is no more work." Here grace and works are absolutely opposed. Although Paul is speaking specifically about election in this context, he is laying down a general principle in his argument which applies to every aspect of soteriology, namely, that which comes as a gift of grace cannot at the same time come because it is earned. Grace and works exclude each other from the doctrine of justification.

*Second*, grace is always coupled with faith and associated with it. What comes to us by grace is received by faith. Ephesians 2:8: "By grace you have been saved through faith." Romans 4:16: "Therefore it is of faith that it might be by grace, to the end that the promise might be sure." Righteousness comes by faith. This is God's way of grace. The promise is appropriated only by faith. And it is sure and certain only when we cling to it by faith and do not trust our works. The Apology argues at length in this vein.

> Forgiveness of sins is a thing promised for Christ's sake. Therefore it can be received only by faith [*sola fide*]. For a promise cannot be received except by faith alone [*nisi sola fide*]. In Romans 4:16 Paul says, "Therefore it is of faith that it might be by grace, to the end that the promise might be sure": as though he were to say, "If the matter were to depend upon our merits, the promise would be uncertain and useless because we could never determine when we would have sufficient merit." Experienced consciences can readily understand this. Therefore Paul says (Galatians 3:22), "God consigned all things to sin, that what was promised to faith in Jesus Christ might be given to those who believe." Here he denies us any merit, for he says that we are all guilty and consigned to sin. Then he adds the promise which is that the forgiveness of sins and justification are given; and then he adds how the promise can be received, namely, by faith. (Apology IV, 84)

On the basis of these two passages which he cites, Melanchthon is arguing that God comes to us with His grace and justification by means of a promise; and there is only one way to respond appropriately to a promise, namely, by receiving the promise in faith.

> Based upon the nature of a promise, this is Paul's chief argument, which he often repeats (Romans 4:16; Galatians 3:18). Nothing one can devise or imagine will refute Paul's argument. So pious men should not

let themselves be diverted from this declaration, that we receive the forgiveness of sins for Christ's sake by faith alone (*tantum fide*). Here we have a certain and firm consolation against the terrors of sin, against eternal death, and against all the gates of hell.

Melanchthon concludes that faith alone justifies because faith alone receives the forgiveness of sins and the Holy Spirit (Apology 46). This is precisely what the Scriptures mean when they testify that we are accounted righteous by faith.[111]

*Third*, the Lutheran Confessions cite the many passages in Scripture which oppose faith to works in the article of justification and which, therefore, prove that justification is by faith alone (Romans 3:28, 4:5-7; Galatians 2:16; Ephesians 2:8-9). These passages contain a variety of phrases and adverbs which exclude good works as playing any role in the justification of a sinner before God. The phrases are "not of works," "without works," "without the works of the Law," "freely," and "it is a gift." These phrases were called "exclusive particles" (*particulae exclusivae*) in our Lutheran Confessions. Paul uses these exclusive phrases and adverbs for the obvious purpose of excluding works from any consideration in the article of justification. To describe the fact that we are justified before God through faith in the saving work of Christ the Reformers used the phrase *sola fide,* a phrase which Luther had already used in his translation of Romans 3:28 (*allein durch den Glauben*) and which became a watchword in the vocabulary of the Reformation. Again we cite Melanchthon's argumentation on this crucial point.

> The particle "alone" offends some people, even though Paul says (Romans 3:28), "We hold that a man is justified by faith apart from the works of the Law," and again (Ephesians 2:8-9), "It is the gift of God, not because of our works, lest any man should boast," and again (Romans 3:24), "We are justified freely by His grace." If they dislike the exclusive particle "alone," let them remove the other exclusive terms from Paul, too, like "freely," "not of works," "it is a gift," etc., for these terms are also exclusive. (Apology IV, 73)

Melanchthon then explains precisely what is being excluded by these phrases. Apparently there had been some misunderstanding on the part of his opponents in regard to this matter. He emphasizes, "It is, however, the opinion of merit that we exclude." The Lutherans are not excluding Word and Sacrament as the means of grace, "For we have said above that faith is conceived by the Word, and we give the highest praise to the ministry of the Word." Also, love and good works are not excluded in the matter of renewal. Love and good works must follow faith and do follow it. But "confidence in the merit of love and of works is excluded in justification." These explanatory words of Melanchthon are very important in clarifying the Lutheran position on the *sola fide*. He wants to make it crystal clear to both Lutherans and their adversaries that the Lutheran doctrine at this point in no way depreciates the means of grace or good works. The *sola fide* is directed to exclude *only* good works in the article of justification, not the grace of God, the merit of Christ, or Word and Sacrament. And the *sola fide* is directed to exclude good works *only* in the article of justification, not in the Christian life of renewal and sanctification.

This explanation of the Lutheran principle of *sola fide* was difficult for Lutherans and Roman Catholics alike to understand and, therefore, to believe. "If works do not help to save us, what are they good for?" it was asked. If the Law does not justify, what good is the Law? Luther railed against this illogical complaint.[112] Hands do not justify, he said. We do not, therefore, cut them off. Eyes do not justify. We do not then pluck them out. Money does not justify. We do not conclude that money is nothing. All these have their proper purpose and use. So does the Law and our good works. The use of the Law is to restrain the wicked and reveal sin. Good works serve God and neighbor. Neither contribute anything to the declaration that a sinner is righteous before God. The hymn stanza of Paul Speratus succinctly and winsomely expresses Melanchthon's explanation of the exclusive *sola fide*.

> Faith to the cross of Christ doth cling
>    And rests in Him securely;
>   And forth from it good works must spring
>    As fruits and tokens surely;
> Still faith doth justify alone,
>    Works serve thy neighbor and make known
>      The faith that lives within thee.[113]

The *fourth* kind of biblical data brought forth to substantiate the *sola fide* consisted of the many Scripture passages which condemn work righteousness and reject the Law as a means of justification. All such passages teach by implication that a sinner is justified through faith alone. In Galatians 2:21 the Apostle Paul says, "If righteousness comes by the Law, then Christ is dead in vain." The righteousness of which Paul speaks comes from God and is the righteousness which avails before God. The burden of the apostle's previous argument was that this righteousness comes to us by faith. The Galatians are, therefore, completely corrupting the Gospel when they teach that righteousness comes to us when we obey the Law. If that were the case, there would be no purpose in Christ's dying, "His death would have been in vain."[114] Galatians 3:10 and Galatians 5:4 are also cited regularly by Lutherans to prove *sola fide* because these verses deny to good works any part in the sinner's justification before God. These passages from Galatians are not just polemical outbursts which have nothing to do with the context of Paul's letter; rather, they illustrate the seriousness of the letter whose theme is justification through faith in Christ without the works of the Law (cf. Romans 3:20). The whole thrust of the Book of Galatians is to show that justification before God is by faith alone.

Roman Catholic theology could accept the principle of *sola gratia* without reservation, according to its understanding of grace and justification; not so in the case of the *sola fide*. The principle of *sola fide* is explicitly rejected by Trent (Ses. VI, chap. 11; canon 9). *The Catechism of the Catholic Church* (1991) teaches that justification is "the acceptance of God's righteousness through faith in Jesus Christ." However, the *sola fide* is clearly not taught when the *Catechism* goes on to say, "Righteousness (or 'justice') here means the rectitude of divine love," and that "with justification, faith, hope, and charity are poured into our hearts, and obedience to the divine will is granted us."

The *sola fide* fits perfectly with all the other elements of the Lutheran doctrine of justification. It does not fit the Roman Catholic paradigm at all. The *sola fide* is the watershed which forms the line of division between Rome and Lutheranism on the doctrine of justification. The *sola fide* is not compatible with Rome's doctrine of habitual grace, justification as a process, *fides formata*, free will, original sin, repentance, good works, and the whole structure of Roman Catholic theology on the article of justification. The Tridentine fathers recognized this fact (Trent, chap. 6, 7, 8).

# Fourteen

# Conclusion: Some Necessary Comments

For almost 200 years, through the period of orthodoxy in the seventeenth century, there had been unity and consensus among the Lutheran churches on the doctrine of justification. The leading confessional Lutheran theologians had deliberately patterned their treatment of the doctrine after the model of the Lutheran Confessions. They had carefully exposed and responded to the errors pertaining to the doctrine, errors already dealt with by the Confessions: Romanism, Majorism, synergism, antinomianism, Osiandrianism. With the advent of the Enlightenment and its offspring (Liberalism, Rationalism, Romanticism, etc.) that close consensus was lost among the Lutheran churches, except in pockets of confessional Lutheranism all over the world, mostly in America. The 1963 Lutheran World Federation (LWF) meeting at Helsinki proved this sorry fact. Consensus on the article of justification simply does not exist today among Lutherans.

After the Helsinki debacle no effort was mounted to regain consensus. The eyes of the Lutheran churches, except for a few smaller confessional bodies, turned toward ecumenical concerns and goals, namely, formal recognition and fellowship with Rome and Geneva. But such recognition and fellowship, if it is to have integrity and stability, must be established on the basis of some kind of minimal doctrinal consensus. This search for consensus has driven all the conversations among Lutherans and Roman Catholics and Reformed Protestants and the many studies and documents resulting therefrom.

Helsinki in 1963 was a signal. The Lutheran churches' inability to find consensus on the article of justification and the relative indifference of the churches belonging to the LWF to follow up on the matter indicated to Rome—and to the Lutheran churches themselves— that future efforts at rapprochement with Rome could be carried out on the basis of minimal doctrinal agreement, or even agreement to disagree. After all, if the Lutheran churches belonging to the LWF could not find consensus among themselves, they could scarcely be expected to find consensus with the Roman Catholic Church as they negotiated toward mutual recognition and church fellowship. Modern efforts to reach mutual recognition and fellowship with Rome on the basis of meaningful consensus were doomed from the start, at least from the side of the Lutherans in the LWF.

This kind of criticism may sound somewhat like poisoning the wells, but the wells were poisoned long ago by the Enlightenment, Rationalism, Liberalism, Modernism, Unionism, and a spate of other movements and heresies with which the Lutheran churches have not been able to cope for the past 200 years, at least not on a confessional basis.

The result of this persisting identity crisis and doctrinal drift among the Lutheran churches is, in their conversations with Rome, the *Joint Declaration* and its proclamation that "a basic consensus between Lutherans and Roman Catholics exists regarding the faith content of the doctrine of justification" (*Joint Declaration*, 42). Whatever differences remain are "compatible with each other."

Clearly, as in the case of the key terms and concepts making up the Lutheran doctrine of justification, the term "consensus" has now suffered severe erosion in meaning. The Augsburg Confession states, "For the true unity of the church it is enough to agree concerning the teaching of the Gospel and the administration of the Sacraments" (VII, 2). And the Formula of Concord (Solid Declaration X, 31) explains that the consensus necessary for church fellowship is "the doctrine of the Gospel and all its articles," no more (ecclesiastical rites, papal authority, etc.), but no less. The consensus of *Joint Declaration* ignores and compromises the confessional Lutheran principle.

Just how did this development happen? At about the time of Vatican II the *modus operandi* for reaching consensus between Rome and the churches of the Augsburg Confession changed radically. From the earliest days of the Reformation the method of dealing with doctrinal differences was polemical in tone and didactic in form. A *status controversiae* was established, and the case of each side was argued according to theses and antitheses. Classic examples of this procedure which emulated the practice of the early church councils (Nicaea, Chalcedon, etc.) were the Formula of Concord and the canons and decrees of the Council of Trent. This method—for it was a distinct, well-defined method—was never used successfully between Lutherans and Catholics after the Reformation, although within each of the two bodies severe doctrinal controversies were settled and consensus achieved. Numerous tracts and enormous tomes were written, affirming the Lutheran and Roman Catholic positions on justification and other articles of faith which divided the two church bodies and refuting the adversary's doctrine on the controverted points. Meetings and colloquiums were held, usually local and only semi-official, where Lutherans and Roman Catholics were located in proximity to each other. But doctrinal agreement was never achieved.

The reason for this failure was not due to a flaw in the tried and true method commonly employed in settling controversies, but to a gradual but inexorable change in the climate and milieu in which theological discussion and attempts to reach doctrinal consensus took place. The failure was due also to a corresponding change in attitude in those who engaged in such discussions. A cultural, religious, and intellectual climate took hold in the nineteenth and twentieth centuries, a climate radically different from that of the sixteenth and seventeenth centuries. If Roman Catholics and Lutherans did not succumb to this *Zeitgeist*, they undeniably were influenced, sometimes heavily, by it.

The predecessors of the Roman Catholics and Lutherans in dialogue today had worked under certain common presuppositions which are no longer taken for granted, even by many who profess to be loyal Lutherans and Roman Catholics. The confessional Lutherans and Roman Catholics of the sixteenth and seventeenth centuries all held that saving doctrine about God and other divine knowledge had been revealed by God to sinful mankind. They all held that this revealed heavenly doctrine was cognitive and capable of being presented in cognitive language. They all believed that revealed doctrine, correctly expressed in creeds and other formulations, was true and, therefore, binding on all Christians. Each side held that the other side taught false doctrine on the issues under controversy.

In the light of these straightforward principles, the method of settling doctrinal controversy mentioned above seemed the only viable and appropriate method, the only possible and honest method of procedure.

The Tridentine fathers and the Lutheran confessors shared another common principle as they tried to cope with false doctrine and settle doctrinal controversy and disputes. They shared the same hierarchy of goals. First and foremost was faithful confession of the *truth* of the divine doctrine, second was *consensus in that doctrine*, and third was *peace* in the church. Their priorities were in that order. This fact can be perceived at once by a reading of the Preface of the Book of Concord (and Preface of the Augsburg Confession, Luther's Preface to the Smalcald Articles, and Preface to the Formula of Concord) and the Bull of Convocation of the Council of Trent under Pope Paul III. There can be no real peace in the church without consensus in doctrine. There is no true consensus in doctrine unless all believe, teach, and confess the same thing, that is, the true doctrine.

Another principle shared by Rome and the Lutheran confessors of the Reformation and post-Reformation era as they strove to confess their faith was that false doctrine must be rejected, not only because such action (confession) is demanded by the First and Second Commandments, but for the sake of the saving Gospel. Theses which asserted the true doctrine must be strengthened, enhanced, clarified, and more effectively communicated by the addition—and sometimes generous addition—of antitheses, often in the form of condemnations.

In recent years this hierarchy of principles has been sometimes ignored, sometimes abandoned, sometimes turned on its head. Thus, Lutherans and Roman Catholics strive today for consensus in doctrine not primarily for its own sake—for the sake of unity in the true doctrine—but for the sake of external unity and external peace among the churches. And consensus becomes a negotiated settlement, a merger and composite of different opinions and emphases, a means to a greater end.

Just this is what has happened in the case of the Roman Catholic/Lutheran dialogues on justification and the statements arising from them (*Joint Declaration* and *Justification by Faith*). They have been ecumenical discussions, discussions entered and carried out according to an ecumenical agenda, an agenda according to which external unity is the priority goal. According to this agenda and modern *modus operandi*, the consensus sought and achieved by the many conversations and resultant statements and declarations is something quite different from the unanimity, the *magnus consensus* of the Augsburg Confession (I, 1) on the articles of faith, quite different from the "unity" (*Einigkeit, Concordia*) affirmed by the Formula of Concord (Solid Declaration X, 31), the unity and agreement "in the doctrine and all its articles," and "concerning the right use of the Holy Sacraments."

If this assessment is correct, then *Justification by Faith* and *Joint Declaration* have succeeded in their ecumenical agenda by failing to reach doctrinal consensus on the article of justification. This failure has already been documented several times in the preceding discussion.

But now a few concluding critical comments are in order.

## 1. Antitheses and Condemnations

As the result of a deliberate decision by Lutheran and Roman Catholic participants in the discussions, *Justification by Faith* and *Joint Declaration* avoided the practice of using antitheses and condemnations as they worked for consensus on the doctrine of justification. There are two reasons for this decision. *First*, it was alleged that the condemnations and antitheses of the Reformation era were often beside the point in that day and simply do not apply in ours. *Outmoded Confessions?* has proven this allegation to be revisionist and, in many cases, contrary to historical facts. *Second*, it was assumed that antitheses and condemnations are no longer useful, but are actually detrimental in achieving consensus on doctrinal points formerly under controversy.

This latter leads to avoiding a practice which was consistently employed not only by the Christian Church for hundreds of years but by the prophets and apostles and by our Lord Himself as they preached the Law and the Gospel. If they had not pointed out and warned against false doctrine, their message would not only have been diluted, it would have been compromised. Are Saint Paul's condemnations in his letter to the Galatians no longer useful? Are the "exclusive particles"—which are certainly implied antitheses—of Paul's writings on the subject of justification ("not of works": Ephesians 2:9; Galatians 2:16; "freely": Romans 3:24; "without the works of the Law": Romans 3:28; "it is a gift": Ephesians 2:8) of no use in our current presentation of the doctrine? Are Lutherans no longer well advised to use these apostolic phrases to support their doctrine of justification simply because they are antithetical *negativa* which condemn a different doctrinal position? Or are we to say that we should no longer apply the Pauline condemnations to modern aberrations and heresies parallel to those in his own day?

In addition to the fact that the present dialogues do not follow the example of Christ and the apostles, there is also a serious methodological flaw in the present practice of eschewing antitheses and historical condemnations in working for doctrinal consensus. To establish consensus after centuries of real doctrinal differences and controversy one must first establish what the differences were all about. The *status controversiae* must be set forth before the controversy can be resolved. And antitheses not only facilitate clarification of the *status controversiae*, but constitute it. The controversy can be settled only by resolving the historical antitheses, not by ignoring them or, as *Justification by Faith* and *Joint Declaration* have done, by attempting to transcend them either by a new way of thinking or by approaching them anew outside of any historical context.

*Outmoded Condemnations?* has pointed out that condemnations play a very different role in Lutheran and Roman Catholic theology. In Roman Catholic theology they are straightforward condemnations of those who hold to false and heretical views, and they call for ecclesiastical disciplinary action, often excommunication. For Lutherans condemnations, or antitheses, were stated for didactic purposes, to mark false and pernicious doctrine and avoid those who propagated false doctrine. In the Lutheran Confessions condemnations were not used to facilitate or govern excommunications or church discipline, which was carried out by the pastor (Augsburg Confession XXVIII, 21). Many of the Lutheran teachers condemned (anonymously) in the Formula of Concord (Flacius, Amsdorf, and even the deceased Melanchthon) were not read out of the church nor excommunicated. At times they were even honored.

Because the purpose of antitheses was didactic for the Lutherans (to clarify and support), the theses and antitheses were stated for the sake of the Gospel itself.[115] They became essential for the presentation of positive theology and the entire theological enterprise—yes, for the correct confession of the Gospel itself. By marking and excluding false doctrine antitheses clarified and supported the correct understanding of the true doctrine.

To avoid antitheses as *Justification by Faith* and *Joint Declaration* have done is an obscurantist and counterproductive practice which can only obfuscate the total presentation of the doctrine of justification. To avoid the use of antitheses and at the same time place two contrary "understandings" side by side as being legitimate insights, approaches, or interpretations of doctrine destroys the very concept of understanding and consensus. Understanding in such a case means no more than a personal, subjective predilection, opinion, or prejudice. It does not make sense—and it is certainly not a reflection of Lutheran or Roman Catholic confessional principle—to assert that two parties have consensus and common understanding while at the same time presenting the two parties as having different and divergent understandings on the same topic. Only by the use of antitheses—statements of what Roman Catholics and Lutherans jointly do not believe, teach, and confess—will the two parties achieve clarity and consensus in the present situation.

## 2. The Historical-Critical Method and Sola Scriptura

Beginning with Helsinki, the biblical basis for the doctrine of justification has been passed by in all the studies and dialogues on the doctrine of justification. This is ironic in light of the fact that *Justification by Faith* and *Condemnations of the Reformation Era* and *Joint Declaration* all stressed breakthroughs and new insights resulting from the use of the historical-critical method. It seems obvious that the virtual triumph of the historical-critical method among many Roman Catholic theologians and among even more of the Lutherans has made a strong impact upon the way in which the conversations concerning justification have turned. If the historical-critical method has demonstrated that there is no theological unity in the New Testament, then the many admonitions in the New Testament to teach the pure doctrine and the stress on the importance of pure doctrine and unity in doctrine (Matthew 7:14, 28:20; John 1:17, 4:23, 8:32; Romans 16:17; 1 Corinthians 1:9; 1 Timothy 4:6, 13, 16; 2 Timothy 3:10, 16; Titus 1:9, 2:1) cannot be applied. If there is no unity of doctrine in the Scriptures, there can be no unity of doctrine in the church, which bases her doctrine on the Scriptures; and all the striving and struggles for unity of doctrine in the past have been unachievable and hopeless quests.

Such a state of affairs understandably affected the Lutheran/Roman Catholic efforts toward consensus. Rather than proceeding from a mutual commitment to the divine origin and authority of Scripture as the source and norm of all doctrine in wending their way toward unity and consensus, the different dialogues began from a common commitment to the Gospel (never clearly defined) and from the different insights, understandings, concerns, and emphases which historically have marked Lutherans and Roman Catholics.

Meanwhile, these understandings, insights, concerns, and emphases were not subjected to the authority of Scripture. In the end, neither side ended up listening to the revealed Word of God. And the possibility that the insights, concerns, understandings, and emphases of either side could be unscriptural and wrong was not considered. Not unexpectedly, the Lutheran principle that all doctrine and practice in the church be subjected to the scrutiny of the Gospel of justification (drawn from Scripture) was not applied.

The neglect of biblical studies in achieving consensus was a much greater concession for the Lutherans than for the Roman Catholics. After all, Luther arrived at his doctrine of justification through his intensive study of the Scriptures, particularly Paul's Epistles to the Romans and Galatians. This was not true of the Roman Catholic adversaries as they tried to respond to him with a coherent doctrine of their own. They went not to the Scriptures only, but to the fathers and scholastic theologians.

The dialogues following Vatican II have clearly followed the Roman rather than the Lutheran approach. And the Lutheran principle of *sola Scriptura* (Formula of Concord, Solid Declaration, Rule and Norm, 3; Smalcald Articles II, II, 15) has been seriously undermined. Coupled with the failure to employ the Scripture principle directly to their various past and present insights, understandings, concerns, and emphases has been the failure of Lutherans and Roman Catholics in dialogue to pay attention to the very learned and convincing lexicographic and word studies, recently written, which have shed light upon the meaning of all the key terms making up the doctrine of justification: sin, repentance, justification, grace, and faith. A perusal of Gerhard Kittel's *Theological Dictionary of the New Testament* clearly establishes the fact that the Lutheran Reformation understanding of all these terms was the correct one. And if that great dictionary had been consulted, many of the basic differences could have been resolved.

One is led inexorably back to a problem already broached several times, the problem of continued equivocation and different meanings attached to fundamental theological terms by Lutherans and Roman Catholics.

### 3. Logomachy and Equivocation

Lutherans and Roman Catholics of the Reformation and post-Reformation eras have been described as battling over words. The portrayal which is usually made to criticize the intransigence of both parties is quite correct. The controversy raging in the sixteenth century as it centered in the doctrine of justification was quite simply a battle over words, a fierce battle over whose meaning and definition should be attached to the words "grace," "justification," and "faith." Each side believed sincerely that this battle over words was the battle for the true theology, and they believed that theology was nothing but words about God. Each side believed also that the battle for words was justified, just as the battle for the iota of the *homoousios* was justified during the Arian controversies in the fourth and fifth centuries. And the outcome of this controversy depended upon whose distinctions and meanings would gain ascendancy.

To this day, after all the many Lutheran/Roman Catholic negotiations and dialogues, the controversy has not been settled, at least not in the sense of unequivocal meanings being attached to the key words making up the doctrine of justification. But there has been a settlement of a different kind. The settlement is an amalgam of the old Lutheran and Roman Catholic definitions, or rather, a pasting together of the two disparate sets of definitions—sort of like a treaty. Neither side gives up its set of definitions and meanings. The treaty provides that the Lutheran and the Roman Catholic will no longer battle over words, meanings, and definitions, but each will keep his own. And this is the agreement, the settlement, the consensus. After four-and-a-half centuries the two church bodies have debated and conversed and fought to a draw. Neither side wins over the other or loses to the other.

### 4. Ecumenical Consensus or Doctrinal Consensus

This, then, is the consensus whereby both Lutherans and Roman Catholics turn away from past controversies and wars over words and join and work together. But it is a consensus diplomatically and politically achieved, a consensus which does not settle or try to settle past disputes, but creates a climate for future cooperation and work. It is a consensus in which Lutherans and Catholics may walk together, not because they are united in the doctrine of the Gospel and all its articles, but because they are united in a common purpose; not because they share a common doctrine (*fides quae creditur*), but because they share a common faith in Jesus and the Gospel (*fides qua creditur*).

Recognizing and understanding such a tense consensus will involve certain risks and compromises, certainly for Lutherans. The Lutheran Church may well have to be prepared to lose its corporate identity sometime in the future, and there may very well be many Lutheran leaders today who are prepared for this eventuality. Or the Lutheran Church may lose its distinctive confession. As observed above, this is already the case in large segments of Lutheranism. Confessional subscription has become very much a *pro forma* custom.

It is important to note that *Joint Declaration* is from the Roman Catholic side a product of an *ecumenical* undertaking. This observation is supported by the fact that it is sponsored by the Pontifical Council for Promoting Christian Unity, not by the Sacred Congregation for the Doctrine of the Faith (the former Holy Office), which is the most important Vatican curial office, charged with the preservation and promotion of Roman Catholic orthodoxy.

If *Joint Declaration*, like its many predecessors, is an ecumenical statement with a definite ecumenical agenda, and not a settlement of previous doctrinal controversies, how is it to be evaluated? How will it be accepted by the Roman Catholic Church and by Lutherans? It has already been accepted by the Pontifical Council for Promoting Christian Unity. But how will that bind the Roman Catholic Church? It is hardly possible that the condemnations of Trent will be excised or withdrawn any more than the anathemas of the Ecumenical Council of Nicaea in 325. Will *Joint Declaration* merely serve as a vehicle for further ecumenical arrangements in the future? It would seem that this is a distinct possibility, but the document will not serve as any kind of doctrinal statement binding on the Roman Catholic Church proclaiming official doctrinal consensus. The LWF member churches, being asked to accept the document by its general secretary, will probably do so. Whether the document will be recognized as a settlement of past doctrinal differences or just a pattern and program for ecumenical relations remains to be seen.

The *Joint Declaration*, then, will have no effect whatsoever upon Rome's official doctrine at any point. Both the decrees and canons of the Council of Trent will remain fully intact and represent Rome's doctrinal position on the doctrine of justification, even if the canons are no longer activated (anathemas have not been in effect for many years).

Meanwhile, the ecclesiastical impediments to fellowship between Rome and the Lutheran churches will remain. There will be no full fellowship until the Lutheran churches recognize Rome's position on many hard issues involving ecclesiology: women's ordination, apostolic succession, papal authority, and church rites (Augsburg Confession VII).

## 5. The Doctrine of Justification and Confessional Subscription

If the major Roman Catholic/Lutheran statements and declarations expended little effort studying and synthesizing the vast biblical data pertaining to the doctrine of justification, they spent just as little time bringing the Lutheran Confessions to bear on the subject. One is particularly disappointed that the theology of the Apology and the Formula of Concord is virtually ignored as the Lutheran "concerns" and "understandings" are rehearsed. This neglect of the theology of the Lutheran Confessions can presumably be explained by the fact that

Trent's treatment of justification is polemical and not didactic in form and is not given to being quoted. And perhaps the Lutheran participants in the dialogues wanted to give equal time to the other side. But any confessional Lutheran will be disappointed, nevertheless, that the two foremost confessional Lutheran presentations of the doctrine of justification played no role in the formulation of the Lutheran position in either *Justification by Faith* or *Joint Declaration*. The confessional Lutheran will conclude that those Lutherans who participated in the final draft of *Justification by Faith* and *Joint Declaration* were not very serious about their confessional commitment.

It goes without saying that confessional subscription to the Book of Concord means that Lutherans take the Confessions seriously, especially what the Confessions say about the subject of justification. Confessional subscription requires that the "pattern of doctrine" of the Lutheran Confessions to which all Lutherans subscribe be used to "judge and regulate" other writings that crop up in the life of the church (Formula of Concord, Solid Declaration, Rule and Norm, 10), especially when pertaining to the doctrine of justification. Confessional subscription means that Lutherans will not deviate from the Lutheran form of doctrine "either in content or formulation" (Preface to the Book of Concord, Tappert, 9), as they enter into doctrinal discussion with those of a different confession, especially when discussing the fundamental article of justification. This commitment to confessional subscription was lacking in the Lutherans who participated in the formation of *Justification by Faith* and *Joint Declaration*.

Such a confessional approach to dialogue with those of different confessions will perhaps seem hopelessly out of date and unworkable today, reflecting an outmoded view toward creedal statements and confessions. But such is the approach of the Lutheran Confessions themselves and should be the viewpoint and position of those who subscribe them.

At this point there is an impasse. For the Lutheran churches to accept *Joint Declaration* as a consensus on the doctrine of justification will not only compromise their witness to the evangelical Lutheran doctrine on justification, but will compromise the confessional principle itself. Most of the Lutheran churches which will be asked to accept *Joint Declaration* will probably ignore or reject this assessment. They will argue—if they are sufficiently interested in doing so—that the confessional principle here enunciated may well be that of the Lutheran Confessions themselves but is, like the condemnations of the sixteenth century, no longer applicable for one reason or another today. In response it must be said that the Confessions themselves make the point that their affirmations and condemnations are *always* applicable (Preface to the *Book of Concord*, Tappert, 8) and that they will stand before the judgment seat of God with their theses and antitheses and give an account (ibid., 9; cf. Formula of Concord, Solid Declaration XII, 40).[116] Of course, many Lutherans will probably disagree with such a position concerning confessional subscription and the confessional principle, even if it is the position of the Confessions themselves. They have long since abandoned such a stand.

And there the matter rests, presumably for a long, long time. In the meantime, one last statement from the Apology of the Augsburg Confession (XX, 7) captures, in one rhetorical question, the spirit of confessional Lutheran witness to the doctrine of justification by faith alone and the urgency of commending this doctrine to the universal church: "Who would not gladly die in the confession of the article that we receive the forgiveness of sins freely given for Christ's sake and that our works do not merit the forgiveness of sins?"

# Notes

## *Abbreviations to Luther's Works*

Reference abbreviations to Luther's writings, except those to the American Edition of Luther's Works, are those employed by Kurt Aland, *Hilfsbuch zum Lutherstudium* (Gütersloh: Carl Bertelsmann Verlag, 1956), 22.

E      Volumes of the German section of the Erlangen Edition.
E ex  Luther's Latin exegetical works in the Erlangen Edition.
WA    The Weimar Edition
LW    The American Edition (Concordia, St. Louis, and
      Fortress, formerly Philadelphia, now Minneapolis)

1.    E Gal, 10, 137; E ex, 21, 20; E ex, 21, 12.

2.    WA, Tr; 1583; LW 54, 157.

3.    WA, 28, 271 ff.

4.    E ex: 21, 3.

5.    WA, 40, 296; LW 26, 176.

6.    Luther spoke indiscriminately of the article of Christ, the article of justification, and the article of faith in Christ as we have seen. This practice was neither deliberate nor haphazard, but natural. Luther and the Lutheran Confessions never considered justification narrowly as a mere formulation or definition. The justification of a sinner, whether considered as an article of faith or an event, cannot be separated from the grace of God, the redeeming work of Christ, the work of the Spirit through the means of grace and faith in Christ. The article of justification entails all these biblical motifs and cannot be presented or confessed in isolation from them. This highly significant fact, so

crucial to the understanding of the Lutheran doctrine of justification, is brought out in all the Lutheran Confessions and writings of Lutheran theologians through the seventeenth century. It is very likely, at least in part, that recent liberal Protestant theologians (Schweitzer, Raven, Deissmann, Wrede, et al), because they ignore this fact, have relegated the doctrine of justification to the periphery of biblical theology and explained away St. Paul's intense discussion of justification as a narrowly focused outburst against the Judaizers. Such a conclusion by liberal theologians may be due as much to a kind of narrow, analytical exegetical method, as to liberal theological propensities. See Henry Hamann, *Justification by Faith in Modern Theology* (St. Louis: Concordia Publishing House, 1957).

Because the Lutheran Confessions and Lutheran theology consistently understand the doctrine of justification in the broad sense as embracing also the doctrine of God's grace in Christ, the person and work of Christ, the means of grace, and the work of the Holy Spirit, they are able to find the doctrine of justification in sections of Scripture and citations from the Church Fathers which do not mention the word "justification" or even its cognates. We note this practice throughout Luther's works, particularly in his *Lectures on Genesis* and his *Sermons on the Gospel of St. John*. On the other hand, Lutheran theology can address the subject of justification without explicitly using the terms "justify" or "justification" by employing other equivalent or interchangeable biblical themes, such as "save," "reconcile," "forgive," and the like. Examples of such a procedure occur in Luther's two catechisms.

7. This is the thesis of Werner Elert throughout his *The Structure of Lutheranism* (tr. by Walter Hansen [St. Louis: Concordia Publishing House, 1962]). Karl Barth, who identifies firmly with Luther's doctrine of justification, is of the same opinion. He says (*Church Dogmatics*, tr. G. W. Bromiley [Edinburgh: T. & T. Clark, 1956], IV, I, 522), "There can be no question of disputing the particular function of the doctrine of justification. And it is

also in order that at certain periods and in certain situations, in face of definite opposition and obscuration, this particular function has brought out in a particular way, that it has been asserted as *the* Word of the Gospel, that both offensively and defensively it has been adopted as *the* theological truth. There have been times when this has been not merely legitimate but necessary, when attention has had to be focused on the theology of Galatians and Romans (or, more accurately, Romans 1-8)." Barth goes on to observe that the doctrine of justification has served this function today. "In the face of all ecclesiasticism, sacramentalism, liturgism, and even existentialism we have been glad enough, and still are, to find in the doctrine of justification a fully developed weapon with which to meet all these things." This complimentary statement does not fully represent the Lutheran view and fails to understand the scope of the Lutheran confessional principle. Barth conceives the function of the article of justification as primarily a corrective function to profess the evangelical doctrine. But at least he recognizes that there is theological validity in the Lutheran principle.

Both Elert and Barth assert that post-Reformation Lutheranism, starting already with Melanchthon, did not follow Luther in his emphasis upon justification and its role in the theological enterprise and the proclamation of the Gospel (Barth, *Church Dogmatics.*, IV, I, 522). So also Alister E. McGrath (*Justitia Dei: A History of the Christian Doctrine of Justification, from 1500 to the Present Day* [Cambridge: University Press, 1986], 51 passim). McGrath is much more dogmatic than Elert or Barth. He says, "Both in terms of its substance and emphasis later Lutheran Orthodoxy (in its doctrine of justification) bears little relation to that of Luther." The same uncritical and cavalier assumption appears in "Justification by Faith," *Lutherans and Catholics in Dialogue VII: Common Statement*, edited by H. George Anderson, T. Austin Murphy, and Joseph A. Burgess (Minneapolis: Augsburg Publishing House, 1985), par. 93. These assertions and assumptions are simply not correct. All this is not so. Martin Chemnitz (and his successors) believes, teaches, and confesses with Luther every aspect of Luther's doctrine. In his *Loci Theologici* and clearly throughout the Formula of Concord he consciously keeps the article of justification central to the preachment and confession of the Church. In his *Loci Theologici* (Wittenberg, 1653, II, 200) he says:

> This article is in a sense the stronghold and high fortress of all the doctrine and of the entire Christian religion; if it is obscured or adulterated or set aside, the purity of doctrine in other articles of faith cannot possibly be maintained. But if this article is kept pure, all idolatry, superstitions, and whatever corruptions there are in other articles of faith tumble down of their own weight.

The later Lutheran theologians echo Chemnitz on the dominant function of the doctrine of justification. Balthasar Meisner (*Anthropologia Sacra* [Wittenberg, 1663], 139) says:

> This article is the central point of theology according to which all the other articles of faith are adjusted; it is the sacred ocean into which all other teachings flow; it is the treasure chest of our faith which keeps safe and unharmed all the other teachings.

And John Andrew Quenstedt, the greatest of the seventeenth century Lutheran dogmaticians, says (*Theologia Didactico-Polemica, sive Systema Theologicum* [Wittenberg, 1685], P. III, C. 8, S. 1, Th. 1, 514):

> This most glorious doctrine of the gracious justification of a sinner before the bar of God through Christ as he is received in true faith is the citadel of the whole Christian religion; it is the nexus by which all members of the body of Christian doctrine are joined; and should this doctrine be violated, all the remaining articles will be abandoned and overthrown.

With the advent of pietism and the Enlightenment Lutheranism has generally lost its appreciation for the centrality and positive role of the doctrine of justification. But there are impressive and notable examples of Lutheran theologians and confessional Lutheran church bodies which have remained faithful to the confessional Lutheran principle.

The present study will be citing rather prolifically many of the great Lutheran teachers through the period of orthodoxy. While such a procedure may lengthen the study, it is necessary to show that confessional Lutherans until the late seventeenth century were remarkably dependent upon Luther and the Formula of Concord in their exegetical and dogmatic writings. The later Lutheran teachers were more than mere stereotypes of Luther, Melanchthon, and Chemnitz. They went to great pains to clarify and support the position of the Formula of Concord. This they did for didactic and polemical reasons, and that in response to Trent and the many Roman Catholic commentators on Trent. This tense situation served to solidify the later Lutherans in their commitment to the Lutheran Confessions, particularly in regard to the doctrine of justification.

8.   There is practically no mention of the concept of justification in H. Denzinger's *Enchiridion Symbolorum* (editio 31, by Karl Rahner [Freiburg: Herder, 1957]). Luther's emphasis was new since apostolic times.

9.   The Council of Trent, which in disposition is polemical and committed to reform, allots a long session to deal with the subject of justification. It does so primarily to substantiate its doctrine of grace, penance, sanctification, and the Sacrament of the Altar. *The Catechism of the Council of Trent*, a summation of the theology of the Council for clergy, didactic in purpose and irenic in tone, appearing first in 1566, does not so much as mention the article of justification. In the three cases where it uses the term "justify" the term means no more than that a person becomes (*fieri*) pious. See *Catechismus ex decreto SS. Concilii Tridentini ad Parochos*, Pii V Pont. Max. jussu editus (Rome: 1566), I, VII, 7; III, I, 8; IV, XII, 10. Thus it reflects the theology of Trent.

10.  A. Tanquerey, *Synopsis Theologiae Dogmaticae Fundamentalis* (Paris, 1925); Ludwig Ott, *Fundamentals of Catholic Dogma* (St. Louis: B. Herder Book Company, 1954).

11.   "On Justification," Document No. 3, Fourth Assembly of the Lutheran World Federation, July 30-August 12, 1963, Helsinki, Finland, Studies and Reports, *Lutheran World*, Supplement to No. 1, 1965.

The most expansive and detailed study and assessment of the Helsinki statement on justification is found in Nestor Beck, *The Doctrine of Faith: A Study of the Augsburg Confession and Contemporary Ecumenical Documents* (St. Louis: Concordia Publishing House, 1987.) Beck also discusses critically the "Leuenberg Concord" of 1973 between Lutherans and Reformed and "The Gospel and the Church" of 1972 sponsored by the Vatican Secretariat for Christian Unity and the executive committee of the Lutheran World Federation (LWF). He also evaluates thoroughly (pp. 151 ff.) the document, "All Under One Christ: A Statement on the Joint Roman Catholic-Lutheran Commission on the AC [Augsburg Confession]" (1980), which presented the conclusion of the commission of the Vatican Secretariat and the executive committee of LWF as they addressed the question of Roman Catholic recognition of the Augsburg Confession as a "catholic" confession. The conclusion, bolstered by a very learned "joint commentary" (Beck, p. 217) written mainly by German Roman Catholic and Luther scholars, was that a "deep consensus" has been reached, but not "total agreement" on the doctrine of justification.

A more devastating, but no less valid, assessment of *On Justification* and the entire Helsinki meeting is given by Carl E. Braaten in *Principles of Lutheran Theology*, Philadelphia, Fortress Press, 1983. Braaten sees the Lutheran Reformation and Confessions, including the doctrine of justification, as now obsolete and irrelevant. The direct opposite position is taken by George Lindbeck and Vilmos Vajta in *The Role of the Augsburg Confession: Catholic and Lutheran Views*, Philadelphia Fortress Press, 1982. The authors simply reject the confessional principle that the article of justification is the *praecipuus locus* of Christian doctrine. Thus they proved Braaten's contention that *On Justification* and the Roman Catholic and Lutheran "convergences" that followed were indeed a fiasco.

12. *On Justification*, 5.

13. "Justification by Faith," *Lutherans and Catholics in Dialogue VII*, edited by H. George Anderson, T. Austin Murphy, and Joseph A. Burgess (Minneapolis: Augsburg Publishing House, 1985), hereafter cited as "JF." The most extensive and perceptive critique of *Justification by Faith* I have found is Rolf Preus, "An Evaluation of Lutheran/Roman Catholic Conversations on Justification" (Fort Wayne, Indiana: Concordia Theological Seminary, 1987, pp. 57-72.)

14. *Justification by Faith*, 118.

15. *Justification by Faith*, 92.

16. *The Condemnations of the Reformation Era, Do They Still Divide?* edited by Karl Lehmann and Wolfhart Pannenberg (Minneapolis: Augsburg Fortress, 1989), hereafter cited as "CRE" or *Condemnations*.

17. *Outmoded Condemnations? Antitheses between the Council of Trent and the Reformation on Justification, the Sacrament, and the Ministry—Then and Now*, by the Faculty of Theology, Georgia Augusta University, Göttingen, tr. by Oliver K. Olson and Franz Posset (Fort Wayne, Indiana: Luther Academy, 1992).

18. Thomas Aquinas, *Summa Theologica*, P. I, q. 22, Art. 1.

19. See Confutatio Pontifica, August 3, 1530 in Michael Reu, *The Augsburg Confession, a Collection of Sources with Historical Introduction.* (Chicago: Wartburg Publishing House, 1930), pp. 349-350. See also *Die Bekenntnissschriften der evangelisch-lutherischen Kirche* (Göttingen: Vandenhoeck & Rupprecht, 1952), 144, footnote 4, hereafter listed as "BELK."

20. Melanchthon is following St. Augustine at this point (*Marriage and Concupiscence*, I, 24, 27).

21. Thomas Aquinas, *Summa Theologica*, III, q. 27, a. 3, 1. BS, 154, footnote 7.

22. *Canons and Decrees of the Council of Trent*, tr. H. J. Schroeder (St. Louis and London: B. Herder Book Company, 1941), hereafter cited as "Trent."

23. See *Melanchthons Werke*, ed. Hans Engelland (Gütersloh: C. Bertelsmann Verlag, *Loci communes*, 1521), II, 1, p. 21.

24. Melanchthon goes on to cite St. Augustine: "That law which is in the members is forgiven by spiritual regeneration, but it remains in the mortal flesh. It is forgiven because its guilt is absolved by the Sacrament that regenerates the faithful. But it remains because there continue to work those desires against which the faithful struggle" (probably Gratian, *Decretum*, III, *De consecratione*, D. 4, c. 2).

25. WA, 18, 600-787; LW 33, 3-295.

26. A quote from Luther, WA 42, 122; LW 1, 163.

27. German: *es sei alles und eitel Sünde mit uns*. Latin: *universam et meram esse peccatum quoad nos et nihil esse in nobis, quod non sit peccatum sive reum*.

28. Melanchthon is echoing the early Luther who stressed that the more faults we see in ourselves, the more abundantly we receive the grace and righteousness of God (WA, 3, 31; LW 10, 34).

29. *Sacrae Theologiae Summa*, Patres Societatis Jesu Facultatem Theologicarum in Hispania Professores (Madrid; Las Editorial Catolica, 1956), 3rd ed., Vol. 3: *de gratia Christi* by Severino Gonzales, 490 ff. The most articulate and penetrating Protestant account of the Roman Catholic doctrine of grace I have found is Karl Barth, *Church Dogmatics*. IV. I, 84-88.

30. See Pohle on "Grace" in *Catholic Encyclopedia*, ed. Charles G. Herbermann, Edward A. Pace, *et al* (New York: The Encyclopedia Press, 1913), VI, 691.

31. See Gonzales, Tanquerey, Ott, and other standard Roman Catholic dogmatics books.

32. *Catechism of the Catholic Church* (Mahwah, New Jersey: Paulist Press, 1991), 2000, hereafter cited as *Catholic Catechism*.

33. See his *Sermo de duplici justitia* (1519), WA 3, 145 ff., where he describes Christ's *justitia aliena* being infused from outside (*infusa extra*). Luther often spoke this way: "When God justifies the ungodly He pours in grace (*gratiam infundit*)" WA 56, 226.

    Again, commenting on Romans 5:15, he says, "The grace of God (by which God justifies us and which is in Christ as its source, just as sin is in Adam as its source) and the gift is that which Christ sends (*diffundit*) from the Father into those who believe" WA 56, 318. In his sermon (1537) for the Nineteenth Sunday after Trinity Luther speaks of God pouring in grace when He forgives sinners ($W^2$ 19, 1722), and in a sermon of 1522 for the First Sunday in Advent he speaks about the "righteousness of God," meaning that "grace and mercy are poured into us through Christ." Luther likes the image of our good and loving God pouring out (or in) blessings upon His children (Large Catechism I, 25). Clearly Luther, like the ancient church collects, in these and other instances is using the image of pouring metaphorically to denote God's beneficent and copious giving of His righteousness or His love or His Spirit or His grace, etc., giving what is His in the first place and comes always from Him.

34. Compare also $W^2$ 11, 1104: "Faith holds out the hand and the sack and just lets the good be done to it. For as God is the giver who bestows such things in His love, we are the receivers who receive the gift through faith which does nothing. For it is not

our doing and cannot be merited by our work. It has already been granted and given. You need only open your mouth, or rather, your heart and keep still and let yourself be filled."

35. *Catholic Catechism*, 1812 ff.

36. WA 39, 99; LW 34, 168.

37. $W^2$ 5, 573.

38. J. H. Schröder, *Eins ist Noth.*

39. Martin Chemnitz, *Examination of the Council of Trent*, tr. Fred Kramer (St. Louis: Concordia Publishing House, 1971), 494 ff.

40. Quenstedt, for instance, gives perfunctory attention to grace as a factor at work in Christ's carrying out His high priestly office. He notes merely that the grace of God is the *causa impellens interna* for the sending of Christ in His mission of redemption (Romans 3:24). See *Systema*, Par. II, C. III, Memb. II, Th. 41 (Wittenberg, 1515 edition; II, 536-537). In fairness to him, however, we should point out that he speaks in a more detailed way about God's love and mercy being the moving cause in God for the saving work of Christ (Romans 5:8; John 3:16, 15:13; Ephesians 2:5). And he stresses that the *causa promerans* of the vicarious satisfaction is the redemptive work of Christ.

41. *Justification by Faith*, 158.

42. None of the "Background Papers" leading to *Justification by Faith*, many of which are excellent and very informative and clear away much misunderstanding of the Roman Catholic and Lutheran positions respectively on justification, touches upon the bitter controversy between Lutherans and Roman Catholics since the Reformation on the nature of grace. This seems strange.

43. Cf. *Condemnations of the Reformation Era*, 18-20, passim.

44. This fact is virtually conceded in two incisive, but largely ignored, books written prior to Vatican II by two Roman Catholic theologians on the biblical meaning of grace. See R. W. Gleason, *Grace* (New York: Sheed and Ward, 1962), and C. Journet, *The Meaning of Grace* (New York: P. S. Kennedy and Sons, 1957). Both scholars lean heavily on the contributions of Gerhard Kittel's *Theological Dictionary of the New Testament* (Grand Rapids, Michigan: Eerdmans Publishing Company, 1964-1976) on the term *charis*, certainly one of the most definitive studies of the term ever made. As far as I can see Kittel and other similar source materials have not been consulted to any extent by the Roman Catholics and Lutherans on the term "grace" or any of the other key words related to the doctrine of justification. The article on *charis* in Kittel clearly supports the understanding of the term "grace" by Chemnitz in his *Examination of the Council of Trent* and in other Lutheran writings of the day.

45. The Formula of Concord takes the same tack. However, the emphasis in Apology IV is on justification *by faith* and the new obedience, or the relationship between justification and good works. The Formula of Concord, on the other hand, while following Melanchthon's approach very closely, is concerned to nail down what is meant by the *righteousness* of faith, or the righteousness which is imputed to the believer in justification. See Solid Declaration III, 30, which says "Scripture teaches that the righteousness of faith before God consists solely in a gracious reconciliation or the forgiveness of sins which is bestowed upon us by pure grace because of the unique merit of Christ, the Mediator, and which we receive only by faith in the promise of the Gospel."

46. Melanchthon points out that not only Paul but also James uses the term in the same sense (*usu*) that a wicked man is "pronounced" righteous (Apology IV, 252).

    That Melanchthon consistently uses the term in this simple and exclusively forensic sense has been disputed in recent times by both Lutheran and Roman Catholic scholars. These scholars tell us that when he says (Apology IV, 117) that in justification we are "made righteous" (ex iniustis iusti efficiamur), the term "justification" denotes more than a divine forensic act, but includes also regeneration and sanctification (renewal), that is an event or process which occurs in man.

47.   Balthasar Mentzer, *Exegesis Augustanae Confessionis (Opera Latina)* (Frankfurt, 1669), I, 60.

48.   Martin Chemnitz, *Loci Theologici* (Frankfurt and Wittenberg, 1653), II, 251.

49.   $W^2$ 13, 2609.

50.   $W^2$ 8, 659-661; LW, 24, 346-348.

51.   WA $40^1$, 285 ff; LW 26, 166-168. Later in his *Lecture on Galatians* Luther, commenting on Galatians 3:13, presents his doctrine of the "blessed exchange" (WA, $40^1$, 443-444; LW 26, 283-284):

> With gratitude and with a sure confidence, therefore, let us accept this doctrine, so sweet and so filled with comfort, which teaches that Christ became a curse for us, that is, a sinner worthy of the wrath of God; that He clothed Himself in our person, laid our sins upon His own shoulders, and said: 'I have committed the sins that all men have committed.' Therefore He truly became accursed according to the Law, not for Himself but, as Paul says, for us. For unless He had taken upon Himself my sins, your sins, and the sins of the entire world, the Law would have had no right over Him, since it condemns only sinners and holds only them under a curse. Therefore He could neither have become a curse nor have died, since the cause of the curse and of death is sin, of which He was innocent. But because He took upon Himself our sins, not by compulsion but of His own free will, it was right for Him to bear the punishment and the wrath of God—not for His own Person,

which was righteous and invincible and therefore could not become guilty, but for our person.

By this fortunate exchange (*feliciter commutans*) with us He took upon Himself our sinful person and granted us His innocent and victorious Person. Clothed and dressed in this, we are freed from the curse of the Law, because Christ Himself voluntarily became a curse for us, saying: 'For My own Person of humanity and divinity I am blessed, and I am in need of nothing whatever. But I shall empty Myself (Phil. 2:7); I shall assume your clothing and mask; and in this I shall walk about and suffer death, in order to set you free from death.' Therefore when, inside our mask, He was carrying the sin of the whole world, He was captured, He suffered, He was crucified, He died; and for us He became a curse. But because He was a divine and eternal Person, it was impossible for death to hold Him. Therefore He arose from death on the third day, and now He lives eternally; nor can sin, death, and our mask be found in Him any longer; but there is sheer righteousness, life, and eternal blessing.

We must look at this image and take hold of it with a firm faith. He who does this has the innocence and the victory of Christ, no matter how great a sinner he is. But this cannot be grasped by a loving will; it can be grasped only by reason illumined by faith. Therefore we are justified by faith alone, because faith alone grasps this victory of Christ. To the extent that you believe this, to that extent you have it. If you believe that sin, death, and the curse have been abolished, they have been abolished, because Christ conquered and overcame them in Himself; and He wants us to believe that just as in His Person there is no longer the mask of the sinner or any vestige of death, so this is no longer in our person, since He has done everything for us.

52. LW 26, 284.

53. George Tavard, *Justification: An Ecumenical Study* (New York: Paulist Press, 1983), 53, passim.

54. Tavard, ibid., 52.

55. Eric Gritsch points out that Melanchthon deliberately formulated Article IV of the Augsburg Confession in such a way as "not to

offend Catholic theologians." Melanchthon does this, Gritsch says, by using the traditional term *"imputat."* See Eric Gritsch, "The Origins of the Lutheran Teaching on Justification" in *Justification by Faith*, 169.

56.  The *Catholic Catechism* takes its doctrine of the nature of justification straight from Trent at this point. *Catholic Catechism*, 1992, passim.

57.  S. Bonaventure, *Commentaria in IV Libros Sententiarum* (in *Opera Omnia*, ad Calaras aquas, 1882-1902, 4 vol.), III, 1, 1.

58.  Chemnitz, op. cit., I, 520.

59.  Kramer, op, cit., I, 532.

60.  See Martin Chemnitz, *Loci Theologici*, tr. J. A. O. Preus (St. Louis: Concordia Publishing House, 1989), II, 475-485; *Examination of the Council of Trent*, I, 469-477, passim.

61.  Robert Bellarmine, *Disputationis de Controversiis Christianae Fidei* (Milan, 1721, de justificatione, I, III). This statement of Bellarmine's became a standard definition for the nature of justification to subsequent Roman Catholics and is quoted also regularly by Lutherans.

62.  *Catholic Encyclopedia*, 6, 692. See also Francis Pieper, *Christian Dogmatics* (St. Louis: Concordia Publishing House, 1950), II, 2.

63.  See John Andrew Quenstedt, *Systema* (Wittenberg, 1702), Par. III, Cap. 3, S. 2, q. 1 (II, 760).

64.  Bellarmine, op. cit.

65.  Quenstedt, Par. III, Cap. 3, S. 1, Th. 12.

66. David Hollaz, *Examen Theologicum Acroamaticum* (Leipzig, 1750), P. III, S. 1, C. 8, q. 18 (P. 927).

67. Gonzales, op. cit., III, 618.

68. See Quenstedt, Par. III, Cap. 8, S. 2, q. 5 (II, 777).

69. WA 39, 97-98; LW 34, 167.

70. Friedrich Balduin, *Commentarius in omnis Epistulas Beati Apostoli Pauli* (Frankfurt, 1710), 78.

71. *Systema*, Par. I, Cap. 8, 5, 2, q. 5 (II, 775 ff.).

72. Ibid., II, 777.

73. Ibid., II, 783.

74. *Systema*, Par. II, Cap. 3, Memb. 2, S. 1, Th. 44 (II, 363). Cf. Abraham Calov, *Apodixis Articulorum Fidei* (Lüneburg, 1684), 249: "Although Christ has acquired for us the remission of sins, justification, and sonship, God just the same does not justify us prior to our faith. Nor do we become God's children in Christ in such a way that justification in the mind of God takes place before we believe." It is doubtful that the Roman Catholics could have made a statement like that of Quenstedt's cited above. In their view Christ merited forgiveness of sin, peace with God, and righteousness, but He did not *acquire* forgiveness and righteousness as *objective realities* which are offered in the Gospel. Righteousness and forgiveness are possibilities which become realities only when the process of justification and sanctification has begun.

75. Luther and the earlier post-Reformation theologians do not present quite such a neat and tidy paradigm, but would probably agree with Quenstedt that Christ procured righteousness on the

cross and that the same righteousness is *apprehended* through faith. All the Lutherans were in agreement that through faith the sinner acquires a righteousness which already exists objectively.

76.   *Systema*, Par. III, Cap. 8, S. 2, q. 5, *Observatio* 19 (II, 787).

77.   *Systema*, Par. III, Cap. 7, S. 1, Th. 19, Note 2 (II, 755).

78.   See Quenstedt, *Systema*, Par. II, Ch. 2, Memb. 2, S. 1, Th. 22 (II, 320).

79.   Luther condemns the scholastic theory thunderously as a denial of Christ and the Gospel. He says:

> There are some within the new academies who say that forgiveness of sins and justification of grace depends entirely on the divine imputation, that is, on God's reckoning; and that it is enough that God imputes or does not impute sins to a person, for in that matter he is either justified or not justified of his sins, as Psalm 32 and Romans 3 speak, 'Blessed is the man to whom the Lord will not impute sin.' If this were true, then the entire New Testament would be nothing and useless. Then Christ worked foolishly and unnecessarily when He suffered for sin. Then God Himself in all this carried out a mock battle and a tricky game (*Kauckelspiell*). For He was able to forgive and not reckon sins without the suffering of Christ. And therefore our faith other than faith in Christ could bring righteousness and salvation, namely, a faith which would rely on such gracious mercy of God which makes one free of sin. Against this miserable and shocking opinion and error the holy apostles have had the custom always to refer to faith in Jesus Christ and to speak of Christ so often that it is a wonder that there is anyone to whom such a cause is not known. Thus, these learned men in the high schools know no longer what Christ is or why He is necessary, or what is meant by the Gospel in the New Testament. They make Christ only a new Moses, a teacher, who gives them new laws and commandments by which man is to become pious and live. (WA 10[1], 469)

80.   The terminology and conceptualization of Melanchthon are just as realistic as the phrase we find in Trent (Ses. VI, chap. 7),

namely, that in justification "an unrighteous man becomes (*fit*) righteous," although Melanchthon is saying that a man is made righteous by imputation whereas Trent says that a man becomes righteous by infusion.

81. J. Perrone, *Praelectiones Theologicae* (Regensburg, 1853), II, 229.

82. Not only Lutheran theologians (Werner Elert, Francis Pieper, and others) have tried to explain the Lutheran/Protestant position, but Reformed theologians have entered the discussion very effectively in recent years. See the excellent treatment of the reality of justification in Karl Barth, *Church Dogmatics*, IV, I, 95. Barth says:

> Certainly we have to do with a declaring righteous, but it is a declaration about man which is fulfilled and therefore effective in this event, which corresponds to actuality because it creates and therefore reveals the actuality. It is a declaring righteous which without any reserve can be called a making righteous. Christian faith does not believe in a sentence which is ineffective, or only partly effective. As faith in Jesus Christ who is risen from the dead it believes in a sentence which is absolutely effective, so that man is not merely called righteous before God but is righteous before God.

Cf. also p. 283. See also G. C. Berkouwer, *Faith and Justification* (Grand Rapids, Michigan: Eerdmans, 1952), 87, passim. Defending both the Lutheran and the Reformed Confessions Berkouwer says, "God does not allow Himself to be either the perpetrator or the object of illusions. His 'reckoning' is worlds removed from make-believe."

83. Not even in the many "Background Papers", which one might assume were used as a basis for the concluding "Material Convergences," is there any mention of an imputation of the *justitia aliena* to the believer, except in a provocative study by

Gerhard Forde entitled, "Forensic Justification and Law in Lutheran Theology" (*Justification by Faith*, 278-303), which seems to have been ignored by the participants.

84. JD includes the Holy Spirit's creation of active love in the believer as a part of justification. This means that God imputes to a believer what he already has by infused grace.

85. Cf. Martin Chemnitz, *Loci Theologici*, tr. J. A. O. Preus (St. Louis: Concordia Publishing House, 1981), which contains not merely Chemnitz' words but also the 1553 edition of Melanchthon's *Loci Communes* (II, 585 ff.).

86. *Loci Theologici*, II, 490 ff.; *Examination of the Council of Trent*, I, 595.

87. *Examination of the Council of Trent*, I, 577.

88. *Loci Theologici*, II, 500.

89. Jesper Brochmand, *Definitiones Articulorum Fidei* (Copenhagen, 1662), A7.

90. Abraham Calov, *Apodixis Articulorum Fidei*, 30.

91. David Hollaz, *Examen Theologicum Acroamaticum*, P. I, S. 2, C. 7, q. 13 (P. 1175).

92. All the Lutheran teachers through the period of orthodoxy consistently set the seat of justifying faith in the intellect and will of man, not his emotions. The pietists stressed increasingly that justifying faith (trust) was an emotion of the "heart," and stressed that this emotion was an experience which a believer could reflect upon and draw assurance from. Nowhere in the Lutheran Confessions is this notion to be found. In the Confessions trust is an activity of the intellect and will of a person, not the "heart." And according to the Confessions and

later Lutheran teachers the heart of a believer is regularly associated with his will. In the Confessions the term "heart" is used for the person of the believer himself, similar to the way the Scriptures employ the terms "heart" and "soul" and "spirit," etc. Thus, the Confessions often speak of the righteousness of the heart (Apol. IV, 265, 371, 373; VII, 36), the sanctified heart (Apol. IV, 189), comfort of the heart (Apol. IV, 62, 80), spiritual influences in the heart (Apol. IV, 125), terrified hearts, hearts that love, renewed hearts, believing hearts, etc.

93. Quenstedt makes the interesting observation:

> There are three parts or activities of faith: knowledge, assent, and trust. According to the first we believe without doubt certain things about God; according to the second we believe without doubt God; according to the third we believe without doubt in God. Heretics can have the first; only the orthodox can have the second; only the regenerate the third. Now the last always contains the first, but the first does not always contain the last. The first two pertain to the intellect, the third to the will. The first two look to the whole Word of God, the last to the promises of grace and the merits of Christ. *Systema*, P. IV, C. 8, S. 1, Th. 5, Nota (II, 1335).

94. Gonzales, op. cit., III, 805; *Catholic Catechism*, 1814.

95. *Systema*, P. III, C. 8, S. 2, q. 1, Obs. 5 (II, 1361).

96. *Examen*, P. III, S. 2, C. 7 (1167).

97. Sebastian Schmidt, *Commentarii in Epistolas D. Pauli ad Romanos, Galatas et Colossenses* (Hamburg, 1704), 380 [commenting on Romans 3:3].

98. Quenstedt (*Systema*, P. I, C. 5, S. 1, Th. 7, note [I, 353]), in discussing the articles of faith in his prolegomena, asserts that justifying faith is trust. A trust in what? Sinful man trusts that God wills to be merciful on account of Christ's merits and to give him as an individual eternal life. Three constitutive articles

play into this trust and underlie it, according to Quenstedt. 1) Trust believes that God is merciful toward fallen man. 2) Trust believes that the merit of Christ and His atonement is for all men; it is universal. "Christ the Redeemer by His total merit and His high priestly office is the meritorious cause of salvation. He alone by His intercession moves our Heavenly Father to be merciful. By His active and passive obedience, carried out for us, He alone pacifies our Heavenly Father and makes expiation for our sins and secures eternal life for us." It is entirely proper therefore that these "benefits" are "confidently embraced" by sinners and "applied to sinners personally with a firm faith." 3) Trust believes that God seriously wills to give salvation in Christ to all and to bestow faith in Christ on all. Thus, trust (*fides justificans*) can and ought to conclude that God has decided (*decrevit*) to give me, the individual, salvation and the faith to receive it. Trust, then, is the "individual application" of the benefits of Christ. It establishes a relationship to God and to Christ, a relationship whereby the sinner is "absolved of sin and declared righteous." Quenstedt makes this same observation throughout his dogmatics book. Cf. P. III, C. 9, S. 1, Th. 11; P. IV, C. 1, S. 1, Th. 17; P. IV, C. 8, S. 2, q. 3.

99.  *Systema*, P. IV, C. 8, S. 2, q. 4, Th. (II, 1362).

100. *Christian Dogmatics*, IV, I, 745.

101. Francis Pieper, *Christian Dogmatics*, vol. 2, 426. Cf. Karl Barth, *Church Dogmatics*, IV, I, 127 ff. Barth refuses to separate the person from the work of Christ and to abstract the person from His work.

102. WA 40[1], 165; LW 26, 88-89.

103. The historic Lutheran position has taken the dative *pistei* as a dative of means, the genitive *dia tēs pisteōs* as an instrumental genitive, and *ek pisteōs* as the genitive of source in an instrumental—never in a causal—sense. In Latin the instru-

mental role of faith in justification was consistently rendered by *per fidem* or the ablative *fide* (thus *sola fide*). In German the phrase is regularly rendered "durch den Glauben." The Lutheran teachers render all three constructions found in the Pauline epistles as instrumental.

If the genitive of source (*ek pisteōs*) of Romans 5:1 and elsewhere in St. Paul's writings is not interpreted as instrumental in the context of justification but causal, then faith is no longer a passive instrument which receives the righteousness of God but becomes itself a cause of justification. If the faith that justifies is not the passive receiving of Christ's righteousness and benefits, but is viewed as some virtue or quality or activity contributed by man which prompts God to justify the sinner, then the genitive of source (*ek pisteōs*) of Romans 5:1, Galatians 2:16, and elsewhere is not instrumental but causal. In effect this would mean that the cause of justification is faith itself; man would be justified not *per fidem* but *propter fidem* and *post fidem*. Faith is then a factor which at least logically precedes justification and becomes a condition for it.

As already noted, Luther spoke of *passiva contritio* indicating that contrition is worked in man by God monergistically through the Word of the Law. Man does not produce his own contrition (Smalcald Articles III, III, 2). So also, Luther says, in the matter of justification and salvation man does not produce his own faith, but faith is worked in man by the Holy Spirit through the Word of the Gospel. Faith behaves in a "purely passive way" (*pure passive*: Solid Declaration II, 89); it receives. Thus, both contrition and faith came to be called an *actio passiva*, an activity of man in which man is not active. It is an activity worked by God in man who is the passive object of a divine action. Man believes, but his believing is a work and gift of God.

Modern linguistic analysis has arrived at the same conclusion as Luther. Based on the deep structure of the verb "believe," the following conclusions have been drawn. Although the verb "to believe" is grammatically a transitive verb, having a direct object (the mercy of God, the forgiveness of sins, Christ, the Gospel) like other transitive verbs, it is not an "action verb" which produces some effect upon its object or affects its object in some way. It is rather a "stative verb," affected or even caused by its object, a verb which points to a state of affairs or a state of being or an ongoing relationship. See the essays by Theodore Mueller: "Repentance and Faith: Who Does the Turning?" in *Concordia Theological Quarterly*, 45:1-2 (January-April 1981); "Justification: Basic Linguistic Aspects and the Art of Communicating It" in *Concordia Theological Quarterly*, 46:1 (January 1982); "Linguistic Nonsense about Faith" in *Concordia Theological Quarterly*, 48:1 (January 1984). Mueller is drawing from the studies of Charles M. Rossiter and W. Barnett Pearce, *Communicating Personality* (Indianapolis: The Bobbs Merrill Co., 1975), 224-234, and other modern linguistic analysts.

The Roman Catholic theologians, following the Vulgate's literal translation of the Greek text, render the three Pauline constructions with *ex fide* or *fide* or *per fidem* (Ephesians 2:8; Romans 3:28 in the case of *dia tēs pisteōs*). It is not clear whether Roman Catholic theology understands the *ek pisteōs* to be instrumental or not. Roman theology would have no trouble with the idea that a sinner is justified "through faith." Rome, however, did not agree with the Lutheran teaching that faith in the article of justification is pure *receptivity* and in that sense is the only means whereby a sinner receives righteousness and forgiveness from God.

104. $W^2$ 9, 1104.

105. Elling Hove, *Christian Doctrine* (Minneapolis: Augsburg Publishing House, 1930), 280.

106. *Systema*, Par. III, C. 8, S. 1, Th. 11, *nota* (II, 743).

107. Cf. Olav Odhelius, *Disputationum Homologeticarum in Augustanam Confessionem prima-sexta* (Uppsala, 1653) 226: "This faith does not justify solely as a quality in us, nor by its own power as our action, nor by any capacity it has to choose; but only organically and relatively insofar as it has to do with its

object, God in Christ, and as it embraces the grace of God and the atonement of Christ." Cf. also Quenstedt, *Systema*, Par. I, C. 8, S. 2, q. 6, obj. dialusis 1 (II, 793): "In the matter of our justification faith ought not be considered as a quality, virtue, or disposition which inheres in us, certainly not as some work of ours, since in the matter of justification faith is opposed to all of our works and qualities (Romans 3:28; Ephesians 2:8; Galatians 2:16), but faith must be considered as centered in the blood of Christ."

108. Jacob Heerbrand, *Disputatio de Gratia* (Tuebingen, 1572), 15.

109. WA 40$^1$, 165; LW 26, 89.

110. Pieper, *Christian Dogmatics*, II, 504.

111. Melanchthon goes on to say: "This is not because faith is a work worthy in itself, but because it receives God's promise that for Christ's sake He wishes to be propitious to believers in Christ and because it believes that 'God made Christ our wisdom, our righteousness, and sanctification and redemption' (1 Corinthians 1:30)." See John Gerhard, *Loci Theologici*, VII, 165. Gerhard quotes Luther tellingly: "God has not dealt with men nor does He deal with men in any other way than through the Word of promise. We in turn can deal with God in no other way than with faith in the Word of promise. Here works don't accomplish a thing, nor is there any need of them. It is with men rather that we deal according to works." (II, Lat. Jen. fol. 280)

112. WA 40$^1$, 476 ff; LW 26, 314 ff.

113. Later generations of Lutherans were compelled patiently to repeat the Lutheran understanding of the *sola fide*. Quenstedt says: "Only that on the part of man which enters into the picture when we consider God justifying him can be said to justify. Thus, we are said to be justified by faith exclusively without the deeds of the Law (Romans 3:28; Ephesians 2:8-9). True, faith is

never alone, never all by itself and isolated from good works, but faith alone apprehends the merits of Christ and it is by faith alone that we are justified." *Systema*, Par. III, C. 8, S. 1, Th. 10, nota 2 (II, 743). Cf. also Jerome Kromayer, *Theologia Positivo-Polemica* (Frankfort and Leipzig, 1711), II, 374: "*Sola fides justificat, sed solitaria non existit.*"

114. One cannot resist quoting Luther as he applies this passage (WA $40^1$, 303 ff.):

> What need does a man have of Christ who loved him and gave Himself for him when without Christ by his own congruent merit he can secure grace, where by his own good works of condign merit he can gain eternal life, and when by actually obeying the Law he can be justified? Thus, Christ with all His benefits is simply taken away and has become utterly useless. Why then was Christ born? Why was He crucified? Why did He die? Why did He become my High Priest who loved me and gave Himself as an inestimable sacrifice for me? Why did He do all these things? Simply in vain, if the sophists are right in what they teach about justification. For then I find righteousness in the Law or in myself apart from grace and apart from Christ.
>
> Shall we tolerate, shall we ignore such a blasphemy: that the divine Majesty who did not spare His own Son but delivered Him for us all was not serious but was only playing when He did these things? Before I would condone this blasphemy, I would see not only the holiness of all the papists and fanatics but the sanctity of all the angels cast into eternal hell with the devil and damned. I wish to see nothing but Christ. He alone must be my treasure, so that all other things are but refuse to me in comparison with Him. He must be such a light to me that, when I seize Him by faith, I know not whether there be Law, sin, or any other righteousness in the world. For what is everything in heaven and earth compared to the Son of God? . . .
>
> What could be a more horrible blasphemy than to make the death of Christ of no value? But this I do, if I wish to keep the Law in order to be justified by it. And to make the death of Christ unprofitable is to make of no account His resurrection, His victory, His glory, His rule, heaven, earth, God Himself and His majesty and all things.

115. See the statement of the Gnesio-Lutherans in the *Protestatio Wimariensium* of September 20, 1557 (CR, IX, 286) as they defend the Gospel motivation for their use of antitheses:

> Now if anybody should say that we are hereby seeking to exalt our name and not what serves the glory of God and the common good of the church, then we confess before God the Lord who also sees and judges the innermost thoughts of all men that from the beginning to the present hour we have sought by our condemnation of all corrupt teachings and now seek nothing else than the preservation of the pure doctrine of the Gospel and the separation of the true church from all other rabble and sects.

Hans-Werner Gensichen correctly says that, as a matter of principle in any confession, "the antithesis exists in fact only for the sake of the thesis and must be used in its service." (See Hans-Werner Gensichen, *We Condemn: How Luther and 16th Century Lutheranism Condemned False Doctrine*, tr. by Herbert J. A. Bouman [St. Louis: Concordia Publishing House, 1967], 209.) Gensichen demonstrates abundantly that such use of antitheses is the practice of the Lutheran Confessions.

116. "Therefore, in the presence of God and of all Christendom among both our contemporaries and our posterity, we wish to have testified that the present explanation of all the foregoing controverted articles here explained, and none other, is our teaching, belief, and confession in which by God's grace we shall appear with intrepid hearts before the judgment seat of Jesus Christ and for which we shall give an account. Nor shall we speak or write anything, privately or publicly, contrary to this confession, but we intend through God's grace to abide by it. In view of this we have advisedly, in the fear and invocation of God, subscribed our signatures with our own hands."